THE COASTAL WAR
Chesapeake Bay to Rio Grande

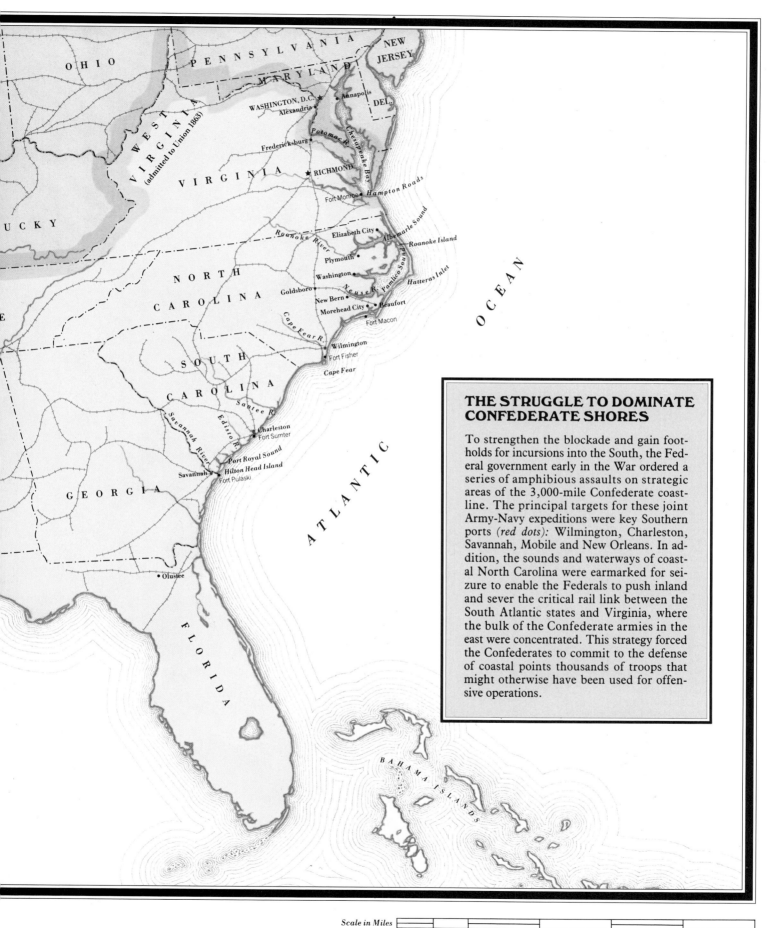

THE STRUGGLE TO DOMINATE CONFEDERATE SHORES

To strengthen the blockade and gain footholds for incursions into the South, the Federal government early in the War ordered a series of amphibious assaults on strategic areas of the 3,000-mile Confederate coastline. The principal targets for these joint Army-Navy expeditions were key Southern ports *(red dots):* Wilmington, Charleston, Savannah, Mobile and New Orleans. In addition, the sounds and waterways of coastal North Carolina were earmarked for seizure to enable the Federals to push inland and sever the critical rail link between the South Atlantic states and Virginia, where the bulk of the Confederate armies in the east were concentrated. This strategy forced the Confederates to commit to the defense of coastal points thousands of troops that might otherwise have been used for offensive operations.

Scale in Miles

0   50   100   200   300   400   500

TIME LIFE BOOKS

Other Publications:

TRUE CRIME
THE AMERICAN INDIANS
THE ART OF WOODWORKING
LOST CIVILIZATIONS
ECHOES OF GLORY
THE NEW FACE OF WAR
HOW THINGS WORK
WINGS OF WAR
CREATIVE EVERYDAY COOKING
COLLECTOR'S LIBRARY OF THE UNKNOWN
CLASSICS OF WORLD WAR II
TIME-LIFE LIBRARY OF CURIOUS AND UNUSUAL FACTS
AMERICAN COUNTRY
VOYAGE THROUGH THE UNIVERSE
THE THIRD REICH
THE TIME-LIFE GARDENER'S GUIDE
MYSTERIES OF THE UNKNOWN
TIME FRAME
FIX IT YOURSELF
FITNESS, HEALTH & NUTRITION
SUCCESSFUL PARENTING
HEALTHY HOME COOKING
UNDERSTANDING COMPUTERS
LIBRARY OF NATIONS
THE ENCHANTED WORLD
THE KODAK LIBRARY OF CREATIVE PHOTOGRAPHY
GREAT MEALS IN MINUTES
PLANET EARTH
COLLECTOR'S LIBRARY OF THE CIVIL WAR
THE EPIC OF FLIGHT
THE GOOD COOK
WORLD WAR II
HOME REPAIR AND IMPROVEMENT
THE OLD WEST

This volume is one of a series that chronicles in full
the events of the American Civil War, 1861-1865.
Other books in the series include:

The Cover: Fires and bursting shells light the surface of
the Mississippi River as a Federal invasion fleet engages Confederate warships south of New Orleans early on
April 24, 1862. At left, the Federal flagship *Hartford*
trades shots with the turtle-shaped ram *Manassas* and
the foundering tugboat *Mosher*.

For information on and a full description of any of the
Time-Life Books series listed on this page, please call
1-800-621-7026 or write:
Reader Information
Time-Life Customer Service
P.O. Box C-32068
Richmond, Virginia 23261-2068

THE
CIVIL
WAR

THE COASTAL WAR

BY

PETER M. CHAITIN

AND THE

EDITORS OF TIME-LIFE BOOKS

Chesapeake Bay to Rio Grande

TIME-LIFE BOOKS, ALEXANDRIA, VIRGINIA

TIME-LIFE BOOKS

EDITOR-IN-CHIEF: Thomas H. Flaherty

Director of Editorial Resources: Elise D. Ritter-Clough
Executive Art Director: Ellen Robling
Director of Photography and Research:
John Conrad Weiser
Editorial Board: Dale M. Brown, Janet Cave, Roberta
Conlan, Robert Doyle, Laura Foreman, Jim Hicks,
Rita Thievon Mullin, Henry Woodhead
Assistant Director of Editorial Resources: Norma E. Shaw

PRESIDENT: John D. Hall

Vice President and Director of Marketing:
Nancy K. Jones
Editorial Director: Russell B. Adams, Jr.
Director of Production Services: Robert N. Carr
Production Manager: Prudence G. Harris
Supervisor of Quality Control: James King

Editorial Operations
Production: Celia Beattie
Library: Louise D. Forstall
Computer Composition: Deborah G. Tait (Manager),
Monika D. Thayer, Janet Barnes Syring,
Lillian Daniels
Interactive Media Specialist: Patti H. Cass

Time-Life Books is a division of Time Life
Incorporated

PRESIDENT AND CEO: John M. Fahey, Jr.

The Civil War
Series Director: Henry Woodhead
Designer: Herbert H. Quarmby
Chief Researcher: Philip Brandt George

Editorial Staff for *The Coastal War*
Associate Editors: Gerald Simons (text); Jeremy Ross
(pictures)
Text Editors: David Johnson, John Newton
Staff Writers: Allan Fallow, Glenn McNatt
Researchers: Kristin Baker, Gwen C. Mullen (principals);
Harris J. Andrews, Brian C. Pohanka
Assistant Designer: Cynthia T. Richardson
Copy Coordinator: Stephen G. Hyslop
Picture Coordinator: Betty H. Weatherley
Editorial Assistant: Andrea E. Reynolds
Special Contributor: Feroline Burrage Higginson

Correspondents: Elisabeth Kraemer-Singh (Bonn);
Margot Hapgood, Dorothy Bacon (London); Miriam
Hsia (New York); Maria Vincenza Aloisi, Josephine du
Brusle (Paris); Ann Natanson (Rome). Valuable
assistance was also provided by:
Juliette Tomlinson (Boston); Carolyn Chubet (New
York).

The Author:
The late Peter M. Chaitin, a veteran freelance writer and
editor, authored or contributed to volumes on a variety of
subjects, including U.S. history and the American Indians. In addition, he was the editor of *James A. Michener's
U.S.A.* and contributed to two previous volumes in The
Civil War series, *Brother against Brother* and *The Blockade*.

The Consultants:
Colonel John R. Elting, USA (Ret.), a former Associate
Professor at West Point, is the author of *Battles for Scandi-
navia* in the Time-Life Books World War II series and of
*The Battle of Bunker's Hill, The Battles of Saratoga, Mili-
tary History and Atlas of the Napoleonic Wars* and *American
Army Life*. He is also editor of the three volumes of *Military Uniforms in America, 1755-1867,* and associate editor
of *The West Point Atlas of American Wars*.

William A. Frassanito, a Civil War historian and lecturer
specializing in photograph analysis, is the author of two
award-winning studies, *Gettysburg: A Journey in Time* and
*Antietam: The Photographic Legacy of America's Bloodiest
Day*, and a companion volume, *Grant and Lee, The Virginia Campaigns*. He has also served as chief consultant to the
photographic history series *The Image of War*.

Les Jensen, Curator of the U.S. Army Transportation
Museum at Fort Eustis, Virginia, specializes in Civil War
artifacts and is a conservator of historic flags. He is a
contributor to *The Image of War* series, consultant for
numerous Civil War publications and museums, and a
member of the Company of Military Historians. He was
formerly Curator of the Museum of the Confederacy in
Richmond, Virginia.

Michael McAfee specializes in military uniforms and has
been Curator of Uniforms and History at the West Point
Museum since 1970. A fellow of the Company of Military
Historians, he coedited with Colonel Elting *Long Endure:
The Civil War Years*, and he collaborated with Frederick
Todd on *American Military Equipage*. He has written nu-
merous articles for *Military Images Magazine*, as well as
Artillery of the American Revolution, 1775-1783.

Library of Congress Cataloguing in Publication Data
Chaitin, Peter.
   The coastal war.
   (The Civil War)
   Bibliography: p.
   Includes index.
   1. United States — History — Civil War, 1861-1865 —
Naval Operations. 2. United States — History — Civil
War, 1861-1865 — Blockades. I. Time-Life Books.
II. Title. III. Series.
E591.C39 1984   973.7'5   84-165
ISBN 0-8094-4732-0
ISBN 0-8094-4733-9 (lib. bdg.)

CONTENTS

Viewed from the mainland, Fort Pickens guards Pensacola Bay in April 1861. The vessel anchored in the harbor is probably a Confederate ship.

Contested Outpost on the Gulf Coast

On April 17, 1861, four days after the fall of Fort Sumter, a U.S. Navy squadron arrived to reinforce one of the last Federal bastions in the South: Fort Pickens, at the entrance to Pensacola Bay on Florida's Gulf Coast.

Three months earlier, Florida troops had occupied Forts Barrancas and McRee on the mainland, seizing the Pensacola Navy Yard along with scores of heavy cannon and tons of ammunition. But Fort Pickens, on a narrow island two miles offshore, held out. And as long as the Federals controlled it, they commanded the best harbor and naval repair yard south of Norfolk.

Once reinforced, the Federals at Fort Pickens grew bolder. Raiding parties destroyed the Navy Yard's dry dock; then a boat's crew from the U.S.S. *Colorado* burned the Confederate privateer *Judah* in the harbor. And in November, Fort Pickens' guns joined those of Federal warships in a barrage that nearly destroyed Fort McRee. By May 1862 the Confederates had abandoned their positions. The Federals reoccupied Pensacola, and it became a base for vital U.S. naval operations in the Gulf.

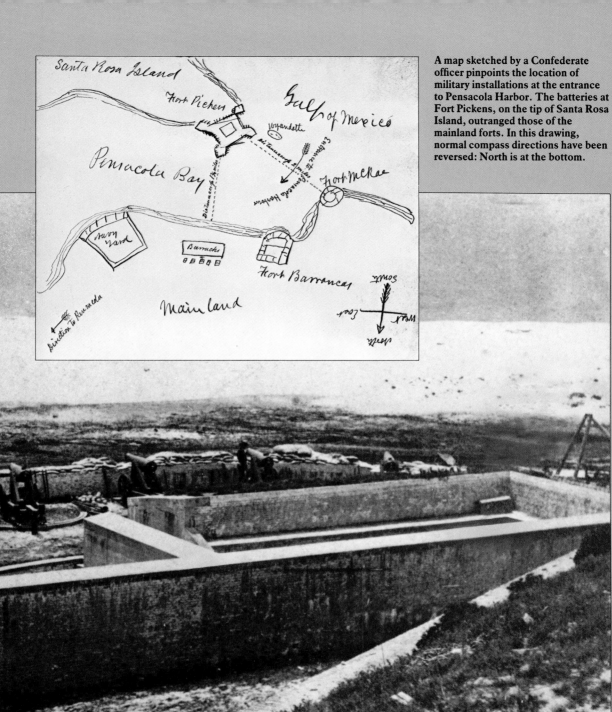

A map sketched by a Confederate officer pinpoints the location of military installations at the entrance to Pensacola Harbor. The batteries at Fort Pickens, on the tip of Santa Rosa Island, outranged those of the mainland forts. In this drawing, normal compass directions have been reversed: North is at the bottom.

Confederates inspect the sea battery at Fort Barrancas in Pensacola Bay. Built around 1840 on the site of a Spanish fort, the battery was outdated by the start of the War.

Two views of Fort Barrancas — one from within — show Confederate artillerymen moving a heavy gun into position across the dry moat separating the main fort from the sea battery. When the Federals evacuated the mainland they spiked the fort's guns, forcing the Confederates to replace many cannon before the batteries could be used.

At Fort McRee, raw Confederate recruits fall in for drill on the parade ground. Most of the Confederate troops at Pensacola were Florida and Alabama men who got their first real taste of war during the confrontation with the Federals offshore.

Southern soldiers assemble for a rare photograph of Confederate camp life. The view depicts many aspects of a bivouac early in the War: from left, boxes of rations, a bugler, a fatigue detail with shovel, and a pipe-smoking officer handing orders to a saluting corporal.

Casually dressed and full of bravado, Confederate recruits drill at their guns in front of a newly constructed battery on the mainland. The green troops learned som

...tter lessons during their stay in Pensacola. Said one soldier, "A man can die and be buried here with the least ceremony and concern I ever saw."

Invading the Inland Sea

"The morn, the fleet, the men, seemed inspired with victory, and moved forward, with the battle half won by their fearless and invincible spirit. It was such a sight as never before disturbed the tranquil waters of America."

PRIVATE WILLIAM P. DERBY, 27TH MASSACHUSETTS, EN ROUTE TO ROANOKE ISLAND

1

All through the summer of 1861, Brigadier General Ambrose E. Burnside was a man in search of a mission. Back in July, the tall, barrel-chested West Pointer had commanded a brigade, including his old 1st Rhode Island Regiment, in the battle at Bull Run. Though the brigade had fought well in that Federal debacle, the troops had seen quite enough of war, and as their 90-day enlistment period expired, most of the men simply packed up and went home. The general was left without an active command.

Burnside kept looking for a chance to serve in some important capacity. Then in October, his close friend and former associate in the railroad business, Major General George B. McClellan, offered him an exciting new assignment, and he jumped at the opportunity. He was to mount an invasion of North Carolina by sea and establish permanent Federal bases for further operations inside the Confederacy.

Both Burnside and McClellan would later claim credit for originating this plan. But the roots of the idea went back several months to the deliberations of the Blockade Strategy Board, composed of Navy and Army officers and the superintendent of the U.S. Coast Survey. As early as June of 1861, the board had begun laying out a general strategy for bottling up Southern ports along the Atlantic and Gulf Coasts.

Initially the board urged the closing off of Hatteras Inlet on North Carolina's Outer Banks. The only inlet on that long sand barrier deep enough to admit oceangoing vessels, Hatteras was the major point of access to the sounds, rivers and ports of North Carolina.

Late in August, forces under Major General Benjamin F. Butler and Flag Officer Silas H. Stringham captured the Confederate forts guarding Hatteras Inlet in the first combined Army-Navy operation of the War. The original plan was merely to block this passage into North Carolina's inland sea, using sunken hulks. However, Butler and Stringham persuaded the Secretary of the Navy, Gideon Welles, to keep the channel open for further operations, leaving a skeleton force of Army and Navy personnel behind to guard it. A more grandiose scheme to invade North Carolina via Hatteras Inlet was opposed by President Lincoln, who insisted that the main business of naval operations on the Atlantic Coast was to blockade Southern ports and establish coaling and supply stations for the Federal fleet. Invasion was to be left to the inland armies.

But General McClellan, the commander of the Army of the Potomac since July, retained an eager interest in the concept of bombardment and invasion by sea; he was predisposed to such operations, having studied the effective use of amphibious operations during the Crimean War. McClellan's thinking influenced the President and the Blockade Strategy Board — in particular Captain Charles Henry Davis, one of the board's two Navy members. The general and the captain dined together in Washington on September 4 and discussed the whole question of invasion by sea. They agreed that, in addition to a planned attack on Port Royal, South Carolina, a special combined force should be sent through Hatteras Inlet to seize the vital North Carolina railroad towns of New Bern and Goldsboro. McClellan then asked Burnside to work out tactical plans for the operations.

Burnside carefully prepared a report that called for a "coast division" of 12,000 to 15,000 men and a "fleet of light-draught steamers, sailing vessels and barges, large enough to transport the division, its armaments and supplies, so that it could be rapidly thrown from point to point with a view to establishing lodgments on the Southern coast." The invading troops would move inland, "thereby threatening the Confederate lines of transportation in the rear of the main army concentrating in Virginia."

Such operations promised another major benefit: support of the blockade of Southern ports. In these early months of the War, the Federal Navy was stretched thin as it attempted to maintain an effective blockade. If Federal forces could capture a sufficient number of major Confederate ports and convert them to U.S. naval bases, the job of the blockade would be made significantly easier; warships would no longer have to absent themselves for long periods to sail back to their remote Northern bases for coal and supplies.

All this dovetailed neatly with General in Chief Winfield Scott's "Anaconda Plan," a proposal to lock the Confederacy in an economic stranglehold by blockading its ports along the Atlantic and the Gulf and cutting off its access to the Mississippi River. In Burnside's North Carolina plan lay the seeds of a modified Anaconda strategy that President Lincoln would adopt, one that stressed the importance of actually seizing Southern ports and railheads, rather than simply blockading them.

The relatively modest operations that Burnside would mount in the autumn of 1861 were to have far-reaching consequences. They would serve as the model for a long series of amphibious assaults demanding close Army-Navy cooperation. In this developing coastal war, Federal forces would launch full-scale assaults against New Orleans, Charleston, Mobile Bay and North Carolina's Fort Fisher, while lesser offensives would be undertaken in the Louisiana bayous and along the Florida coast.

On January 7, 1862, after months of preparation, McClellan formally authorized an amphibious assault on 12-mile-long Roanoke Island, nestled between the North Carolina coast and the Outer Banks. Several ports nearby on the mainland were earmarked for occupation as well.

Roanoke Island was a logical choice as an attack site. Having seized Hatteras Inlet, south of Roanoke Island, the Federals had access to the entire sweep of Pamlico Sound. To the north, the Confederates still held Albemarle Sound, a 60-mile-long waterway cutting into the North Carolina coast. The bulwark that separated Pamlico Sound from Albemarle Sound was Roanoke Island, and the Confederates had fortified it heavily. The capture of this island would eliminate the Confederate threat to Federal operations along coastal North Carolina and give the Federals great flexibility of movement. Troops could land and advance northward

As troops of Major General Benjamin Butler wade ashore at Cape Hatteras, North Carolina, on August 28, 1861, a U.S. Navy flotilla under Flag Officer Silas Stringham bombards the Confederate Forts Hatteras and Clark. This first Federal combined operation resulted in the capture of the forts, along with 670 prisoners, 1,000 small arms and 35 cannon.

against Norfolk and its vital naval base, or southward against the railhead at New Bern and the rail junction at Goldsboro. If Goldsboro could be captured, the railroad supply line from the deep South to Richmond — and the Confederate Army in Virginia — would be severed.

In writing his report, Burnside had discreetly refrained from asking for troops from McClellan's carefully husbanded Army of the Potomac. Instead, he sought volunteers from the seacoast towns of New England and the Middle Atlantic states. He proved to be an eloquent recruiter. Volunteers began to arrive at Annapolis, Maryland, in late October of 1861, and by early January some 13,000 recruits — hardy souls from New Jersey, Pennsylvania, New York and New England — were taking part in intensive training.

Though they did not yet know it, these men were destined for Hatteras Inlet. The recruits were to rendezvous at Fort Monroe on the Virginia Peninsula with a Navy flotilla of 20 hastily improvised gunboats under the command of Flag Officer Louis M. Goldsborough and proceed to Hatteras in a convoy. Many of Burnside's new soldiers were drawn from the ranks of fishermen and merchant sailors. Oddly, it was their knowledge of ships and the sea that led to the campaign's first crisis.

As the men began embarking at Annapolis for the journey down the Chesapeake to Fort Monroe, they quickly lost the enthusiasm they had shown throughout their training period. They were worried by the prospect of an ocean voyage on their motley fleet of 60-odd river barges, sailing vessels, commercial steamers and armed tugs. The main trouble with these vessels was their

Toehold at Port Royal

In late October of 1861, a massive fleet of 66 warships and transports carrying 12,000 troops set sail from Fort Monroe with orders to secure Port Royal Sound, a strategic anchorage midway between Charleston and Savannah. Though the Federal ships were scattered by a gale off Cape Hatteras, all but four managed to rendezvous opposite Forts Walker and Beauregard, strongholds guarding the approaches to the sound.

At 9:30 a.m. on November 7, fifteen warships under Flag Officer Samuel F. Du Pont steamed into the sound. General Thomas Drayton, the Confederate commander at Port Royal, noted that there was "not a ripple upon the broad expanse of water to disturb the accuracy of fire from the decks of that magnificent armada." The ships sailed around the bay in an ellipse, riddling the two forts with up to 24 shells per minute. The rounds fired by the frigate *Wabash*, reported a shipboard observer, kicked up pillars of smoke on shore that looked "as if we had suddenly raised from the dust a grove of poplars."

The Confederates gamely returned fire, but found their armament unequal to the task. Some guns were fouled by outsized shells, bowled over by their own recoil, or blown apart by defective fuses; several batteries simply ran out of ammunition. Worst of all, the enemy's circling tactic deprived the gunners of fixed targets.

Within five hours the defenders were fleeing to the mainland. General Thomas Sherman's forces then landed to take over the forts. Private Charles Caldwell marched with the Federals into Fort Walker to discover that "many of the dead were half buried where they fell; guns were dismounted, army wagons smashed. Knapsacks, blankets and rifles lay in confusion all around."

In a year of demoralizing defeats for the Federals, the seizure of Port Royal Sound helped revive Northern spirits. The U.S. Navy had secured a choice supply base for its blockading squadron, and the Army now controlled a string of coastal islands from which it could threaten the Confederate interior and additional strongpoints along the Atlantic shore.

Federal soldiers and sailors give three cheers as the Union standard replaces South Carolina's palmetto banner over Fort Walker on November 7, 1861.

draft: They drew no more than eight feet of water, which was supposed to enable them to cross the swash, or sea-washed sandbar, at the entrance to Pamlico Sound. But these shallow-draft ships could easily founder in the gales so common along the Atlantic Coast. The men were convinced that their lives were at risk.

Before setting out from Fort Monroe, General Burnside made a dramatic gesture to quiet the grumbling of his men. His own quarters were aboard the *George Peabody*, one of the largest and safest of the transports. He immediately transferred to the tiny armed steamer *Picket*, the smallest vessel in the flotilla.

On the night of January 11, the transports put to sea, and Burnside's show of confidence was soon put to a severe test. Fierce gales off Cape Hatteras whipped the waves into towering walls of water. Wallowing in the troughs, buffeted by wind and water, the diminutive *Picket* appeared doomed. As Burnside reported, "Men, furniture, and crockery below decks were thrown about in a most promiscuous manner. At times it seemed the waves, which appeared mountain high, would ingulf us, but the little vessel would ride them and stagger forward in her course."

Fortunately for the expedition, the *Picket* stayed afloat, and no men were lost. But foul weather stalled the convoy for many days; word of its approach soon filtered to the Confederates along the coast, who had already been alerted to the possibility of a Federal attack.

As things turned out, surprise was unnecessary. To oppose the Federals' armada of warships and the 13,000 troops, the Confederate commander in the region, 55-year-old Brigadier General Henry A. Wise — a former governor of Virginia — had only about 1,400 men on Roanoke Island. Wise's sole reserves were 800 troops stationed at Nags Head on the Outer Banks, and the 700 men of the 2nd North Carolina Battalion en route from Norfolk.

To make matters worse, Wise had little in the way of artillery. Three forts — Bartow, Blanchard and Huger — had a total of 25 guns covering the channel along the west coast of Roanoke *(map, page 26)*. On the mainland, across the narrow Croatan Sound, a barge mounting seven guns had been hauled up on the mud flats and given a plucky name, Fort Forrest. This makeshift strongpoint posed a threat to hostile ships sailing up the western channel, which had been partially blocked by a line of sunken hulls and pilings.

The island's east coast had just two guns, mounted near a place called Ballast Point. The low and marshy southern end of the island was undefended. But in the narrow middle of the island, stretching across the only north-south road, the defenders had an 80-foot-wide redoubt manned by about 1,000 troops and bolstered by one howitzer on the west end, another in the center and a field gun on the east end. The trees before this redoubt had been cut down to provide the defenders a clear field of fire for 700 yards, and the strongpoint was flanked on both sides by a dense, apparently impassable cypress swamp. To capture the position, Federal troops would have to move up the north-south causeway in the face of artillery and small-arms fire from the Confederate breastworks.

The Confederates could expect little defensive help from a fleet of eight small work

U.S. Army troops at Annapolis embark on transports in early January 1862 for the expedition to Roanoke Island. It took more than three days to load the 13,000-man force onto vessels, and though their mission was supposed to be a closely guarded secret, Southern newspapers had in fact already published the destination by the time the ships left port.

boats that had been converted to gunboats by Flag Officer William F. Lynch. General Wise contemptuously referred to them as a "mosquito fleet," and the name stuck. With only one 32-pounder per ship (save for the C.S.S. *Sea Bird,* which boasted two guns), this flimsy flotilla could do little more than sting the 64-gun Federal fleet, and it would run the constant risk of being wiped out by the enemy's firepower.

The Confederate defenses would hardly daunt a determined, well-armed and far more numerous foe, and General Wise knew it. He bombarded authorities in Richmond with appeals for further reinforcements — to no avail. Confederate Secretary of War Judah Benjamin argued that little could be spared without seriously weakening the Confederate battlefront in northern Virginia.

The only person who was in a position to offer Wise real assistance was his immediate superior, Major General Benjamin Huger, District Commander at Norfolk. It happened that Huger had 13,000 idle men at his disposal. But he turned aside his subordinate's request for aid with the haughty recommendation that Wise should demand "hard work and coolness among the troops you have, instead of more men."

Meanwhile, the Federals were having difficulties of their own. Strong winds continued to pound the fleet, forcing the ships of the convoy to wait at Hatteras Inlet for calm seas before negotiating the treacherous passage into Pamlico Sound. Burnside wrote later: "Many of the vessels were driven from their anchors and grounded on the swash and the bar. Many collisions occurred, which caused great damage to the fleet. At times it seemed as if nothing could prevent general disaster."

As the days passed, conditions became close to unbearable on board the troop transports. A captain of the 10th Connecticut noted in his diary: "The skies black; the surf beating sullenly the solemn requiem of the lost; epidemics rapidly extending; deaths frequent; no comforts for the sick; scanty food for the well; water tainted with kerosene, served out in limited quantities." Some shipboard entrepreneurs sold rain water, scooped up from the decks, for as much as 75 cents a cup.

Then, as the weather calmed toward the end of January and Flag Officer Goldsbor-

ough began to pass the ships through the narrow inlet, he and Burnside discovered to their consternation that, contrary to all reports, an eight-foot draft was too deep by about two feet to clear the sandbar. Even when the heavily laden transports were lightened by loading their men and cargoes onto small boats, many vessels could not make it past the bar.

For a time it appeared that the entire expedition might have to be scrapped. But a solution was found: A few of the largest transports were deliberately driven onto the swash under a full head of steam, then held in place by tugs and anchors as the tide coursed under them, digging out the sand beneath their keels. Again afloat, they were

The steamer *City of New York*, laden with guns, ammunition and $200,000 worth of supplies, founders on the bar at the entrance to Hatteras Inlet on January 13. The ship's captain and crew clung to the rigging for almost 40 hours before lifeboats from the other Federal vessels could make their way through the breakers to effect a rescue.

driven on farther into the sandbar and the process was repeated until, foot by painful foot, a deep channel was cleared and the flotilla began to enter the sound. It was not until February 4 that the last of the transports cleared the bar.

Once inside the sound, the convoy was again beset by rough weather. But finally the sun came out, and by February 7 the Federal ships had made their way to Roanoke Island. That morning, the gunboats formed their battle line to begin a bombardment of Fort Bartow, the southernmost of the strongpoints on the west side of the island. Strung out behind the Navy vessels were Burnside's troop transports and supply ships. Aboard the *Picket,* signal flags broadcast a message that paraphrased Lord Nelson at the Battle of Trafalgar in 1805: "Today, the country expects every man to do his duty."

In the western channel, seven of the tiny Confederate gunboats made a menacing show from behind a barrier of sunken pilings. In fact, Flag Officer Lynch had decided not to attack; he would conserve what little strength he had by trying to lure on his foe. If the Federal ships blundered into the obstructions in the channel, their maneuverability might be reduced and Lynch's mosquito fleet might make itself felt. If the Federals got through the obstructions, Forts Blanchard and Huger on Roanoke's west coast and the beached barge Fort Forrest on the mainland could catch the enemy flotilla in a cross fire.

At about 11:30 a.m., Flag Officer Goldsborough's gunboats opened fire on Fort Bartow, situated just south of the sunken pilings. As they pounded away at the strongpoint's earthen walls, the vessels hugged the shoreline so that the Confederates there could bring only three of eight guns to bear.

While the U.S. Navy kept the defenders busy, the U.S. Army prepared to land its troops. A young slave who had recently escaped from a Roanoke Island plantation had provided Burnside with what the general called "most valuable information as to the nature of the shore of the island." Burnside decided to land his troops at Ashby's Harbor, about two miles south of Fort Bartow, and he dispatched his topographical engineer in a boat with a small party of soldiers to inspect the site and take soundings. Though fired on from shore as they made ready to leave, the scouting party escaped and reported that conditions were favorable for a landing.

At about 3 p.m., large longboats were lowered, filled with troops and towed by shallow-draft steamers toward the shore, with each steamer pulling 20 boats. Close in, the steamers veered off sharply, sending the string of landing craft shoreward with the motion of a cracking whip. The towlines were cut and the oarsmen rowed swiftly to the beachhead, grounding the boats on the swampy coast.

It was the first large amphibious landing of the War, and a signal success. In less than an hour 4,000 troops had waded ashore in precise brigade order, and by midnight 10,000 men in blue were on the beach at Ashby's Harbor, making temporary camp in a chilling rain and preparing for the next day's test of arms.

At the same time, two miles to the north, Goldsborough's gunboats continued to pound Fort Bartow. The mosquito fleet twice ventured out from its position behind the sunken pilings, trying to draw the enemy ships north toward the guns of Forts Huger,

Flag Officer Louis M. Goldsborough was a seasoned Navy man whose career began at the tender age of seven, when he was commissioned as a midshipman. In 1861, the Navy ignored a regulation mandating his retirement after 45 years' service and appointed him commander of the North Atlantic Blockading Squadron; the following year, he led the U.S. fleet in the attack on Roanoke Island.

Brigadier General Ambrose E. Burnside, who commanded the Federal land forces at Roanoke Island, had left the Army in 1853 to manufacture breech-loading carbines in Rhode Island. When the firm failed after four years, the genial Burnside took a job with the Illinois Central Railroad, where he cultivated the friendship of its president, fellow West Pointer George B. McClellan.

Blanchard and Forrest. The Federals refused to be distracted, and they pummeled the Confederate fleet. The C.S.S. *Forrest* was hit and retired from the fight, and a shell from the U.S.S. *Southfield* crashed through the C.S.S. *Curlew*, forcing its captain, Commander Thomas Hunter, to ground his ship lest she sink. Unfortunately for the defenders, Hunter beached his foundering craft on the mainland coast, directly in front of Fort Forrest — thus blocking the aim of the fort's gunners.

Now the important action shifted to Burnside's troops entrenched ashore. The general had three brigades, under the command of Brigadier Generals John Parke, John Foster and Jesse Reno. Burnside called them "three of my most trusted friends," and he left the implementation of his plan in their hands while he remained in his headquarters on the island.

Burnside's plan called for the brigades to advance on the Confederate redoubt, with Foster attacking first along the causeway, and Parke and Reno following through the swamp on either side to outflank the Confederates. Foster's brigade would bear the brunt of the enemy's fire. But the men on the flanks would have no easy task; they would have to struggle through brambles and knee-deep mud.

On the morning of February 8, the Federal brigades got into position down the causeway and moved out. As Foster's column, led by the 25th Massachusetts, moved up the road, it was met by a hail of Confederate small-arms and artillery fire. The Federals crept forward painfully, and in their wake they left a litter of wounded and dead. It soon became clear to Foster that his frontal attack would not carry the works, and he ordered

This period map shows the position of the opposing forces at Roanoke Island during the Federal assault on February 7, 1862. While U.S. Navy gunboats confronted the Confederate fleet near Fort Bartow, transports two miles to the south debarked some 10,000 Federal troops at Ashby's Harbor. The next day the soldiers advanced northward in three columns.

NOTE.

Fort Huger is furnished with complete furnaces for heating shot.

Many of the Rebels escaped through Shallowbag Bay and some from the upper end of the island in boats.

Scale of miles.

Navy vessels crowd the waters off Roanoke Island on the afternoon of the Federal invasion. The landing took nearly nine hours and employed more than 60 transports and hundreds of ship's boats.

the 23rd and 27th Massachusetts to march off through the swamp on the right and try to turn the Confederates' left flank.

At about 11:30 a.m. the 25th Massachusetts, having sustained heavy casualties and depleted its ammunition, was ordered to fall back. Its place in the vanguard was taken by the 10th Connecticut. The Connecticut men pushed forward under heavy fire that killed the regiment's commander, Colonel Charles L. Russell.

When the 10th had advanced to within a quarter mile of the Confederate breastworks, Foster called upon Colonel Rush C. Hawkins' 9th New York Zouaves to take the lead and launch a final charge. The Zouaves saw some grim scenes as they moved up the causeway. Private Charles Johnson reported: "As soon as we struck the road, a narrow one, we had to form in ranks of two, in order to let the string of wounded men pass on their way to the rear. This was indeed a ghastly spectacle for us to face on the way to our maiden fight. The poor fellows were in every imaginable condition of bodily suffering; some of them walking bravely or indifferently by themselves with only slight wounds, others supported by comrades, pale as death from loss of blood; still others carried on stretchers, evidently in their last struggle; and some quite still — were they already dead?"

On the Federal left, Reno's men, slogging through the swamp, were having a difficult time getting to the Confederate breastworks. Sergeant George Washington Whitman, the brother of poet Walt Whitman, recalled that his regiment, the 51st New York, worked around on the Confederate right flank "through a thicket that you would think it was impossible for a man to pass through. It

Outfitted in blue-and-red Zouave uniforms, Colonel Rush C. Hawkins (*front row, second from left*) and his staff gather for their portrait in New York before departing for North Carolina in 1861.

The Disputed Triumph of the 9th New York

The motto of Colonel Rush C. Hawkins' 9th New York Volunteers, a Zouave regiment, was *Toujours Prêt* — Always Ready. So when the unit arrived in front of the main Confederate strongpoint on Roanoke Island in February 1862, they were prepared to obey the order: "Now is the time; you are the men. Charge the battery!"

"Both wings of the regiment rushed on together," recalled Sergeant J. H. Whitney of Company B. "They soon reached the moat filled with water, into which they sprang and began climbing up the enemy's battery." By the time they gained the parapet of the battery, however, the defenders had fled. The 9th planted its banner atop the captured works.

Forever after, the proud Zouaves would insist that they had carried the day for the Federals. But other units, which had entered the enemy redoubt from the flank, hotly disputed their claim. "With our own two flags in plain sight upon the parapet," wrote Captain Charles Walcott of the 21st Massachusetts, "the 9th New York came running up and with a great shout of Zou! Zou! swarmed into the battery for all the world as if they were capturing it." A private in the 23rd Massachusetts flatly called the 9th's charge "humbug."

But to a Northern press hungry for heroes, the colorful Zouaves were the men of the hour. Their exploits were celebrated in newspaper articles, sketches and engravings — many of which were wildly exaggerated.

The controversy endured long after the War. Colonel Hawkins stoutly defended the role his men played at Roanoke Island. When a 10th Connecticut man publicly suggested that the Zouaves had actually retreated at the critical moment, Hawkins retorted: "A more baseless slander was never written."

Some light was thrown on the squabble by newspaper artist Frank Vizetelly. A veteran war correspondent who witnessed the assault and produced one of the few accurate depictions of the engagement (*right*), Vizetelly confirmed that other Federal units entered the redoubt before the 9th. Yet he was impressed by the pluck of the Zouaves. He told Hawkins after the battle that the charge of the 9th "was the finest thing I have ever known of a new regiment, and I congratulate you on being its commanding officer."

An inaccurate engraving of the battle on Roanoke Island *(left)* portrays the 9th New York fighting atop the enemy battery. In fact, as depicted below by artist Frank Vizetelly, Federals charging from the left had raised the U.S. flag over the parapet before the Zouaves reached it.

was mighty trying to a fellow's nerves, as the balls was flying around pretty thick, cutting the twigs off overhead and knocking the bark off the trees all around us, but our regiment behaved finely." The New Yorkers did not fire their weapons, Whitman noted, "for fear of shooting our own friends, as we could not see 10 yards on either side."

When finally the Confederate redoubt came into view, Reno gave the order to charge. "Away we went," Whitman wrote, "the water flying over our heads as we splashed through." When the defenders saw the Federal force bearing down on them from the right and realized that they were outmanned, they fled in disarray, leaving behind their dead and wounded, three artillery pieces, and piles of discarded baggage. The 21st Massachusetts and the 51st New York planted their flags atop the Confederate breastworks.

The flanking movement on the left had succeeded in clearing out the Confederates before the Zouaves made their frontal assault. But the Zouaves were unaware of the fact. Chanting their strange battle cry, "Zou! Zou! Zou!" they raced toward the enemy positions and cascaded over the Confederate breastworks. But they found no one to bayonet; the foe had already departed. The Zouaves and their flamboyant Colonel Hawkins would nonetheless stubbornly maintain that it was their own charge that had put the Rebels to flight.

The breaking of the line across the causeway shattered any hopes the Confederates had of holding Roanoke Island. The defenders on the northern tip of the island were trapped, and within hours most of them had surrendered. Some managed to escape in small boats to the mainland or to Nags Head on the Outer Banks. One of those left behind, mortally wounded, was General Wise's son, Captain O. Jennings Wise of the 46th Virginia.

The Federals took 2,500 prisoners. Most of them were soon released, however, since there was no means of maintaining prisoners on the island. They were transported to the North Carolina mainland and paroled on their pledge to take no further part in the hostilities. It turned out that the Confederates, having fought from entrenched positions, had lost only 23 men killed and 58 wounded. The Federals counted 37 dead and 214 wounded.

News of the victory at Roanoke Island was greeted with jubilation throughout the Union. Editor Horace Greeley wrote in his New York *Tribune*, "It now requires no far-reaching prophet to predict the end of this struggle." The Rhode Island legislature proudly dispatched a ceremonial sword to its adopted son Burnside.

The Confederacy responded with bitterness and gloom. The Richmond *Examiner* called the loss of Roanoke and its defending force "certainly the most painful event of the war." The Congress in Richmond launched an investigation and fastened the blame on two men: General Huger, who had denied Wise the reinforcements he needed, and Secretary of War Judah Benjamin, who had had no reinforcements to send. Huger, after another lackluster performance, this time on the Peninsula, would be relieved of his command and transferred to the West. Benjamin was forced to resign his post, but immediately assumed the position of Secretary of State at the insistence of President Davis.

With Roanoke Island taken, the Federal

The *Sea Bird*, flagship of the Confederate "mosquito fleet," goes down in the Pasquotank River near Elizabeth City, North Carolina, during the one-sided battle with warships of the Federal fleet. The Federals took just half an hour to cripple the Confederate flotilla, losing only a few men in the process.

threat to the North Carolina mainland became palpable. Burnside's troops were still mopping up when, on the 9th of February, 14 Federal gunboats entered Albemarle Sound and steamed up the Pasquotank River toward Elizabeth City, where Flag Officer Lynch had sought refuge with the six remaining vessels of his mosquito fleet. Upon learning that the Federal flotilla was approaching, Lynch made hasty preparations to defend himself.

Lynch led his fleet a short distance down the Pasquotank to Fort Cobb, which mounted four 32-pounders. Across the river from this strongpoint he moored the schooner *Black Warrior*, fitted with two guns. Now any Federal vessel pushing upriver toward Elizabeth City would have to negotiate a Confederate cross fire. Just above Fort Cobb, Lynch lined up the other five gun-

boats, stretching them across the Pasquotank to block the river. It was the best Lynch could do, and he only hoped that his pitiful supply of ammunition would hold out.

Commander Stephen C. Rowan, who was in command of the pursuing Federal ships, also needed ammunition badly: He had only 20 rounds per gun. In the interest of conserving powder and shot, Rowan pronounced his mission a "reconnaissance in force," to be converted into an attack on the mosquito fleet only if prospects looked favorable. No firing would be permitted, he wrote in his official report, "until the order was given, and in order further to economize on ammunition, I directed that each vessel as she approached the enemy should run him down and engage hand-to-hand."

Evidently, Rowan decided that conditions for an attack were favorable, for at dawn on

February 10, he ordered his flotilla into battle formation and moved upriver. At about 8:30 a.m., the Federal ships began to close on the enemy. The Confederate ships and the guns at Fort Cobb opened fire at long range and did no damage. Following orders, the Federal ships made no reply until they were almost within hailing distance of Fort Cobb. Now Rowan signaled, "Dash at the enemy!" Throttles open wide, guns spitting fire, the ships steamed between the fort and the ineffectual *Black Warrior* with little difficulty. Soon the Federal flotilla had passed beyond the fort's field of fire; the vessels could now fire with impunity on the strongpoint.

Realizing that his situation was hopeless, the commander of the fort ordered his guns to be spiked and his flag struck, and the position was abandoned. The officers and crew of the *Black Warrior* set fire to their ship and fled ashore.

Continuing full speed ahead, Rowan's fleet ran smack into the five Confederate mosquitoes blocking the river above Fort Cobb. The U.S.S. *Commodore Perry*, under the command of Lieutenant Charles W. Flusser, peeled off to attack Lynch's flagship, the *Sea Bird*. "I fired a nine-inch shell at her," wrote Flusser, "which struck her amidships at the water line, passing through her as if she was so much paper. I then called away boarders and ran for her, my men picking up their muskets, pistols, cutlasses for a hand to hand fight. When fifty yards or more from her, she hauled down her flag and her commander appeared on the upper deck to signify that he had surrendered."

Flusser now shouted orders to avoid ramming the *Sea Bird*, but in the excitement and confusion his helmsman did not hear him.

Brigadier General John Foster, who commanded the Federal center in the battle for Roanoke Island, had been chief engineer of the Charleston Harbor defenses before Fort Sumter fell. In July 1862 he was promoted to major general and named commander of the Department of North Carolina.

The two ships collided, and the *Sea Bird* began to go under. Flusser's men jumped on board the *Sea Bird* and, he wrote, "I had to follow to restrain them from injuring the prisoners. While I was at anchor engaged in taking the prisoners from the sinking vessel, two small rebel steamers ran around us, firing with musketry. I could have sunk them both with one gun, but my men were so wild that I could not get them to their quarters at the great guns."

Meanwhile, a Confederate shell hit the U.S.S. *Valley City*, setting fire to a locker containing ammunition. When the ship's captain went to help squelch the blaze, he found one of his crewmen, quarter gunner John Davis, sitting calmly on an open barrel

Brigadier General Jesse Reno led the triumphant left wing of Burnside's army on Roanoke Island. He later fought under Burnside at the Second Battle of Bull Run and served with McClellan's army in Maryland until he was killed at South Mountain in September 1862.

An able engineer-soldier, Brigadier General John Parke had never led troops in battle before being assigned to command the Federal right wing on Roanoke. His skillful performance in that campaign earned him a promotion to major general.

Federal transports convey Burnside troops up the Neuse River the eve of the Battle of New B in March 1862. The calm s and brilliant weather led one sol to liken the fleet to "summ steamers with excursionist of gunpowder, shielding its contents from the flames. The fire was extinguished before it could reach the explosives, and the heroic sailor was later awarded the Congressional Medal of Honor.

Despite the spirited Confederate resistance, the battle was a walkover for the Federals. Within minutes, the *Sea Bird* was sunk, the *Fanny* was set afire by its own crew to avoid capture, and the *Ellis* was seized in one of the last successful boarding operations in naval warfare. Only the *Beaufort* and *Appomattox* escaped. The *Beaufort* made her way up the Pasquotank to Dismal Swamp Canal and thence to Norfolk, but the *Appomattox* was scuttled by her crew when she proved 2 inches too wide to enter the narrow canal. The Confederate Navy in the sounds

of North Carolina had ceased to exist. The way lay open for Burnside to work his will on the mainland.

Even as Burnside regrouped his forces for the next major operation, joint Army-Navy raiding parties were probing up the rivers along Albemarle Sound to clear out any remaining Confederate defenses. On February 10, within hours of vanquishing the mosquito fleet, Rowan reached Elizabeth City. There he found a crowd of jubilant blacks and a number of burning buildings, put to the torch by white inhabitants before they fled. But the departing townspeople had overlooked a storehouse filled with food. Rowan confiscated the provisions for his men, some of whom he left in Elizabeth City as an occupying force.

Other raids soon followed. On February 19, Commander Rowan led eight gunboats up the Chowan River toward Winton, a village of 300 inhabitants. The flotilla carried 1,000 troops — Colonel Hawkins' 9th New York Zouaves and the 4th Rhode Island Infantry. The Federals intended to destroy two railroad bridges and contact the local pro-Unionists, rumored to be a powerful faction in the area.

Anticipating an attack, the Confederates laid a trap. Near Winton, on a bluff overlooking the Chowan, they secreted a four-gun battery, backed by the 1st Battalion of North Carolina Volunteers. As Rowan's flagship, the *Delaware*, approached Winton, it was awaited by a black woman, who waved a handkerchief as if to indicate that the town was undefended and safe to enter. She had been sent there by her master, a Confederate officer, to lure the ships close in; once near the shore, the Federals would not be able to elevate their guns enough to fire at the Confederates atop the bluff.

The ploy almost worked. Rowan rounded the bend in the Chowan, spied the lady and, reassured by her smiles and beckonings, made for a landing. But at the last moment Colonel Hawkins, who had climbed up in the rigging of the *Delaware*, spotted the glint of Confederate muskets on the bluff. "Ring on, sheer off, rebels on shore!" Hawkins yelled to the helmsman. As the *Delaware* changed course, the Confederates opened fire. "Before we passed out of range," wrote Hawkins, "the low guards, wheel house and masts of the *Delaware* were riddled." Aware now that they faced considerable resistance, the Federals withdrew downriver to reconsider the situation.

That night the citizens of Winton celebrat-

Lieutenant Frazar Stearns, 21-year-old son of the President of Amherst College, was twice wounded at Roanoke Island and barely recovered in time to join his 21st Massachusetts in the fight for New Bern. In the lead when the 21st charged a key Confederate battery early in the battle, Stearns was shot dead — the first of his regiment to fall.

ed, believing that they had routed the foe. But early the next morning the Federal flotilla again steamed round the bend and, from midstream, pulverized the Confederate positions. Then Hawkins and his troops were put ashore to clear the town.

Infuriated by the previous day's trickery, Hawkins ordered Winton burned. Federal troops surged through the streets, torching public buildings, churches and houses. A Federal added in a letter home, "You may be sure that we gave Winton a pretty good ransacking while the flames were doing their work."

The Federal raids on small river ports preceded General Burnside's next major offensive — against the city of New Bern, up the Neuse River from Pamlico Sound. New Bern, on the river's west bank, was the second largest port on the North Carolina coast. Its loss would be a stunning blow to Confederate morale. Once in Federal hands,

New Bern would be a marshaling point for drives up and down the coast and inland along the Atlantic & North Carolina Railroad toward the vital junction at Goldsboro. There, the line from New Bern intersected with the Wilmington & Weldon Railroad, which carried vital supplies to Richmond and points north.

After the fall of Roanoke Island, Confederate forces at New Bern girded themselves for an attack. Under their commander, Brigadier General Lawrence O'Bryan Branch, a 42-year-old Princeton graduate and former congressman, they worked around the clock to bolster the city's defenses. By the second week in March a line of log-and-earth breastworks was established downriver from the town. From Fort Thompson, on the west bank of the Neuse, the line extended westward for about two and a half miles to a two-gun battery on the edge of a swamp along Brice Creek. Manning the defense line were approximately 4,500 green North Carolina troops, including seven infantry regiments, two dismounted cavalry companies and some artillery.

The defenders, expecting that the main attack would come by water, had trained 10 of Fort Thompson's guns on the Neuse River, leaving only three to command the landward approaches. The river had also been liberally salted with torpedoes — as floating mines were then called — and sunken obstructions.

The center of the Confederate line was bisected by railroad tracks built on a causeway. By these tracks, at an old brick kiln, the line skipped northward for 150 yards to pick up the path of a small creek, a natural defensive obstacle, before continuing westward. Branch had not fortified this break in the line, apparently thinking that the defenders within the brickyard would be sufficient to withstand an attack. But here was the weak link in his otherwise well-prepared defenses. The brickyard was held by a small battalion of militiamen who were ill trained and ill armed.

On March 11, General Burnside, with about 11,000 troops, sailed from Roanoke Island to rendezvous near Hatteras Inlet with 13 war vessels of the Federal fleet, led by Commander Rowan. That evening Burnside informed his men that they were about to embark on a great offensive in support of General McClellan's forthcoming invasion of the Peninsula and drive on the Confederate capital.

Everything seemed to favor Burnside's combined operations plan. The link-up with the Navy was made on time, and the flotilla got under way with few delays. Even the notorious coastal weather cooperated. For once, the waters were calm, and as the vessels steamed up the Neuse estuary under a bright sun, the expedition seemed more like an outing than a prelude to combat.

Early on the morning of March 13, the Federal troops disembarked unopposed at Slocomb's Creek, 16 miles below New Bern. By sundown the column had advanced to within two miles of the Confederate defense line, and here they bivouacked for the night in a driving rain.

The foul weather made it impossible to bring forward any artillery except some light naval howitzers. Nor was there any reserve ammunition on hand. Burnside's men would go into battle with only 40 rounds in their cartridge boxes.

At daybreak, in a thick mist, Burnside gave the order to advance. The three gen-

erals who had led their men to victory on Roanoke Island were again in command. Foster advanced with his brigade on the right, Reno came up on the left, and Parke took the center, with his troops ready to assault the Confederates head on or shift to either flank should that seem advantageous. In the meantime, the Federal fleet moved up the Neuse to bombard Fort Thompson in support of the ground forces.

Foster's brigade moved through a forest in front of the Confederate left flank. It was as "quiet as the morning of a New England sabbath," recalled a soldier in the 10th Connecticut. At about 8 a.m., as the Federal troops neared the Confederate breastworks, the silence was broken by a thunderclap of artillery. The rippling crackle of musketry then spread along the opposing lines from the railroad to the river. Foster's five regiments were brought to a standstill, hit not only by enemy fire, but by the shells of the Federal fleet. Commander Rowan, en-

thusiastically peppering the Confederate defenses from the Neuse, later attempted to justify his indiscriminate shelling: "I know the persuasive effect of a 9-inch shell," he commented, "and thought it better to kill a Union man or two than to lose the effect of my moral suasion."

With Foster's brigade pinned down, the action shifted to General Reno's brigade left of the railroad tracks. Lieutenant Colonel William S. Clark, whose 21st Massachusetts was on the right of Reno's line, recalled, "The battle was now raging fiercely upon our right. The smoke from the rapid firing of more than thirty cannon and several thousand muskets was driven down upon us by the wind, and mingling with the dense fog, so completely shut out the light of day that it was impossible to derive any information respecting the position of the rebels except where it was indicated by the noise of battle."

As the 21st Massachusetts blundered

ahead, the men came up against the militia unit holding the brickyard at the railroad tracks. Taking the lead himself, General Reno led four companies of the 21st into the brickyard, scattering the Confederate defenders, who sent up a cry that they had been flanked. The 35th North Carolina, occupying the entrenchments adjacent to the brickyard, were hit on their right flank and fell back in disarray.

But Reno's success was short-lived. Other Confederate regiments held firm and began firing into the Massachusetts men. Lieutenant Colonel Clark reported, "We were subjected to a most destructive cross-fire from both sides of the railroad, and lost a large number of men in a very few minutes." General Branch then sent in the 26th and 33rd North Carolina, who regained the lost ground.

With the remainder of Reno's brigade pinned down on the left, and Foster's brigade stalled on the right, Lieutenant Colonel Clark called on the vanguard of Parke's brigade for help. Colonel Isaac P. Rodman of the 4th Rhode Island responded immediately. He led his own regiment and the 8th Connecticut in a charge that swept through the brickyard, threatening the Confederate left wing.

Outflanked and short of ammunition, the entire Confederate line began to disintegrate. General Branch, realizing the futility of attempting to hold off the Federals, ordered a retreat over the Trent River Bridge to New Bern.

Quickly the retreat turned into a race for sanctuary. A Confederate officer recalled, "Every man struck out for the bridge as fast as his legs would carry him and the additional spur from bombs crashing through

the timber put them to top speed for a three mile sprint." Many of those troops who made it to New Bern headed straight to the railroad depot and scrambled aboard a westbound train, which as luck would have it, was just pulling out.

Branch made no further attempt to defend the town but ordered his regimental commanders west to Kinston, where he hoped to regroup and oppose the next Federal advance. In the fight for New Bern, the Federals had lost 90 killed and 380 wounded. Confederate casualties were lighter — 64 killed and 101 wounded. But 413 Confederates were missing; according to Branch, about 200 of them were "prisoners and the remainder at home."

As the Confederates evacuated New Bern, the Federals moved in, led by Rowan's gunboats, which lobbed a few warning shells into the city before tying up at the docks. Just as at Winton, Rowan found a city from which virtually all but the blacks and the poorest whites had fled. When he asked an elderly black woman where all the Confederate troops were, she replied, "Running as hard as they can."

About a month after New Bern fell, the Federals attacked Fort Macon, at the southern end of Pamlico Sound. The fort guarded the water approaches to the ports of Beaufort and Morehead City, the terminus of the Atlantic & North Carolina Railroad. The Confederates surrendered Fort Macon after a four-day siege. Soon other small cities and river ports along the Pamlico and Albemarle Sounds were taken by Federal troops and gunboats.

These losses quickened the sense of urgency among Confederate authorities over the peril in North Carolina. Shortly after the fall

of New Bern, General Robert E. Lee, then the military adviser to Jefferson Davis, had warned the President that another disaster in North Carolina "would be ruinous." Lee's admonition produced results. By the end of March, thousands of North Carolina troops commanded by Major General Theophilus H. Holmes were pouring into the state to meet Burnside's anticipated drive on Goldsboro. Burnside, meanwhile, was girding his troops for the thrust inland to that town and its rail junction.

But it was not until late June that Burnside received orders to move on Goldsboro. His troops were just about to set off when he received a startling and laconic message from President Lincoln. "I think," the Chief Executive wrote, "you had better go with any reinforcements you can spare, to General McClellan." General Lee, now in command of the Confederate army before Richmond, had thwarted McClellan's advance on the capital. The issue now was not whether McClellan could take Richmond but whether his defeated forces would have to be withdrawn from the Peninsula.

On Bogue Banks off the North Carolina coast, Federal troops under General John Parke attack Fort Macon on April 25, 1862. The troops brought heavy siege mortars and 30-pound Parrott guns to within a mile of the fort and, along with U.S. warships, bombarded the stronghold for 10 hours, causing the 400-man Confederate garrison to surrender.

Accordingly, on July 6, 1862, Burnside and 7,000 of his men took ship from North Carolina to go to McClellan's aid. But soon after they reached Fort Monroe, Federal strategy changed again. In August, McClellan's forces were withdrawn from the Peninsula, and Robert E. Lee advanced northward. After marking time for nearly a month at Fort Monroe, Burnside was dispatched to reinforce Federal troops blocking Lee in northern Virginia.

Though a force of about 8,000 Federals remained in eastern North Carolina, the major Federal offensive there had lost its momentum. Years of raids and counterraids would now be North Carolina's lot, with neither side gaining a decisive advantage. Yet if Burnside's campaign in North Carolina had failed to achieve all its objectives, it had provided the Federal forces with a thorough rehearsal in joint Army-Navy operations, a rehearsal that would prove valuable during the bolder and bloodier coastal offensives that lay ahead.

New Englanders on a Carolina Beach

COLONEL JOHN H. JACKSON WITH STAFF AND SERVANT

Among the thousands of Federal soldiers who occupied Hilton Head Island, South Carolina, in November 1861 were the jubilant men of the 3rd New Hampshire Volunteers. "To plant our feet on the other fellows' heath was exhilarating," wrote Captain Daniel Eldredge, "and the boys capered about like young colts."

Indeed, for men who had rarely ventured more than 30 miles beyond their New England hometowns, the new duty seemed to promise an exotic vacation. Hilton Head's balmy weather contrasted pleasantly with the chilly autumns up North, and the island supported a lush growth of orange and fig trees, palmettos,

and live oaks draped with Spanish moss. The troops feasted on peanuts and yams and helped themselves to the chickens, geese, pigs and cattle they found wandering on the island's abandoned plantations. Soldiers slept on beds of soft, raw cotton in campsites decorated with cactus, driftwood and sea shells.

The New Hampshire men discovered in time that service on Hilton Head was not an unblemished sojourn in paradise. They worked hard building fortifications and a wharf, where they unloaded mountains of supplies. "Instead of the rifle and bayonet," a colonel recalled, "shovels and wheelbarrows came into active and extensive use." The soldiers also battled sand fleas that were so thick they could streak a man's trousers black as he walked through the dunes.

Even so, few could quarrel with the routine on Hilton Head Island. The soldiers found themselves with enough spare time to read newspapers and books, write letters, play dominoes and card games, and listen to serenades performed by the regimental band.

They also received visitors from New Hampshire, among them photographer Henry Moore, whose views of the 3rd Regiment's camp life at Hilton Head appear on these pages.

SURGEON ALBERT MOULTON, HIS WIFE AND YOUNG SON

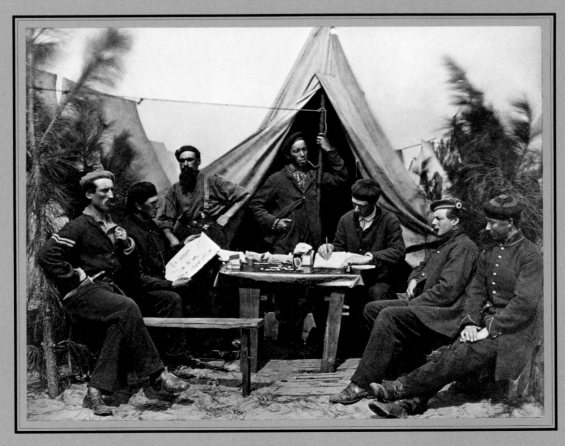

SEVEN MEN OF COMPANY A

BANDMASTER WITH MUSICIANS AND SERVANT

THE REGIMENTAL BAND

DOMINOES AT THE QUARTERS OF CAPTAIN WIGGIN

QUARTERS OF LIEUTENANTS ALLEN AND CODY

A Bid to Cut Off Savannah Harbor

On a November day in 1861, General Robert E. Lee and Colonel Charles Olmstead stood on a rampart of Fort Pulaski at the mouth of the Savannah River and assessed the threat from Tybee Island, clearly visible a mile to the south. Should the Federals place guns on Tybee, Lee told the fort's commander, "they will make it pretty hot for you with shells, but they cannot breach your walls at that distance."

The Union's Captain Quincy Gillmore, a brilliant engineering officer, thought otherwise. In February and March of 1862, troops under Gillmore grappled 36 siege guns and mortars — some weighing eight and a half tons — into positions on Tybee's

Viewed from Tybee Island, Fort Pulaski stands riddled with craters after the Federal bombardment on April 10-11, 1862. The gunners concentrated their fire o

north shore. The men worked by night and concealed their progress with bushes and marsh grass.

At 8:15 a.m. on April 10, Gillmore's guns opened fire, raising puffs of yellow dust where the shells struck Fort Pulaski's walls. Inside the stronghold, Colonel Olmstead recalled, "shots were shrieking through the air in every direction, while the ear was deafened by the tremendous explosions." The U.S. Army's remarkable new rifled guns inflicted the most damage; their high-speed conical shells blasted holes two feet deep in the seven-foot-thick masonry.

By noon the next day, the Federals had opened two yawning gaps in the rampart, exposing the fort's magazine, with its 400 kegs of black powder, to direct shellfire. Faced with annihilation, the 385-man garrison surrendered at 2 p.m. Fort Pulaski, once regarded as impregnable, had succumbed in just 30 hours, and with its capture the U.S. Army sealed off the crucial harbor of Savannah.

...e southeast corner of the fortress, smashing open the casemates *(inset)* with 110,643 pounds of shot and shell.

Inside one of Fort Pulaski's breached casemates, a Federal soldier stands by a 32-pounder smoothbore gun. The Confederate defenders, wrote U.S. Army Lieutenant Horace Porter, had replied actively to the attack, their shots flying about the Tybee Island batteries "like a swarm of bees." Still, not one Federal gun was hit.

At right, a 10-inch seacoast mortar, knocked backward off its base by a direct hit from one of 5,275 shells fired at the fort, lies muzzle down on the shattered southeast rampart. The 8-inch columbiad at left below had been tilted upward in an attempt to lob shells into the Federal trenches and batteries on Tybee Island. The Federals' accurate fire silenced 16 of the defenders' 20 guns.

Federal soldiers repairing the damage to Fort Pulaski pause on the parade ground in April 1862. The Confederate defenders, as ordered by General Lee in 1861, had

erected heavy timbers against the interior walls to shield the casemates and officers' quarters from shell fragments; the ditches had been dug to trap rolling shot.

Months after the Federal assault, Company H of the 48th New York Volunteers stands stiffly at attention inside Fort Pulaski, whose walls and parade ground have been restored to their original condition. Off-duty soldiers in the background play baseball, a favorite pastime among the Federal occupiers of the fort.

The Fight for New Orleans

"The attention of the Navy Department was intently directed toward New Orleans, the most important place in every point of view in the insurrectionary region."

GIDEON WELLES, U.S. SECRETARY OF THE NAVY

New Orleans, brimming with gaiety and optimism in normal times, was not itself in the winter of 1862. The city — by far the biggest in the South, with a population of 168,000 — had suffered much since the start of the War, and new troubles loomed larger with every passing day.

First, U.S. warships had arrived to close the several mouths of the Mississippi about 100 miles south of New Orleans. The naval blockade had grown ever more effective as 1861 wore on, stifling the rich international trade of the Confederacy's premier port. The miles of city docks and levees, formerly lined with tall-masted ships and crowded with stevedores loading cotton and sugar and rice, were now practically deserted. Wrote New Orleans author George Washington Cable: "The city that had once believed it was to be the greatest in the world, was absolutely out of employment."

Worse than the blockade was the growing certainty that the Federals intended to attack New Orleans to open the whole length of the Mississippi to their own commerce. In the Gulf south of Biloxi, Mississippi, on barren Ship Island, a Federal army had been building up for months, posing a threat to New Orleans, Mobile and the Texas coast. And a much more powerful force was apparently New Orleans bound. To the north, an army under Brigadier General Ulysses S. Grant and a river flotilla commanded by Flag Officer Andrew Foote were pushing southward through Tennessee, driving back the army of General Albert Sidney Johnston. During February, the forces of Grant and Foote dealt the Confederates a terrible blow, capturing Forts Henry and Donelson. The fall of these crucial strongholds added no little to New Orleans' jitters.

In hopes of bolstering morale in the city, Louisiana's Governor Thomas Overton Moore called for a grand parade there to celebrate George Washington's birthday. The spectacle had mixed results, however. More than 25,000 militiamen marched, among them units representing many of New Orleans' colorful ethnic groups, and the sheer size of the turnout gave a sense of security to undiscerning spectators. But knowledgeable observers realized that this supposed show of strength actually revealed a glaring weakness: The majority of the troops were unarmed. In fact, supplies were so short that only 6,000 of the men carried a weapon of any sort.

Nevertheless, New Orleans was not without resources, and efforts to improve the city's defenses were vigorously pursued. At key points well below New Orleans, rafts were built and piled high with tar-rich wood. In case of an attack by river from the south, these rafts would be set afire and cut adrift to raise hob among the enemy fleet.

In Jefferson City, just above New Orleans, work was proceeding on two monster ironclads. The *Mississippi* was designed to be the strongest and swiftest warship afloat. Displacing 4,000 tons and carrying three

The wooden gangway board of the *Hartford*, Captain David G. Farragut's flagship for the New Orleans expedition, features a carved seal of Hartford, Connecticut. The city's name derived from the scene depicted — a hart fording a stream.

inches of armor and 20 big guns, she would operate at the remarkable top speed of 14 knots. And the *Louisiana*, a 264-foot ironclad with a 62-foot beam, would be scarcely less formidable.

Great deeds were expected of these ships. Already, the improvised ironclad *Manassas* had proved the value of armor; along with some small wooden vessels, she had surprised and routed a much stronger Federal flotilla of wooden ships at the Head of the Passes in the Mississippi delta, sending the enemy vessels scurrying for the safety of open water. Now it seemed quite possible that the vaunted *Mississippi* and *Louisiana* could smash the blockade, then proceed upriver to wipe out Foote's flotilla — if the pair was completed in time.

Seventy-five miles below New Orleans, facing each other across the Mississippi, stood the two mighty strongholds that constituted the city's chief defense: Fort St. Philip, a citadel built by the Spanish in the 1790s and expanded two decades later; and the more powerful Fort Jackson, a modern pentagonal structure. Brigadier General Johnson K. Duncan, in command at both forts, worked his men furiously to strengthen his positions. Massive iron chains, supported by firmly anchored cypress rafts and floating hulks, were stretched across the Mississippi just south of the forts and well within range of their guns. If Federal ships attempted to run the forts, this barrier would hold them under a devastating cross fire from Duncan's strongpoints, to whose arsenals nine cannon and five seacoast mortars were being added. For further protection, Duncan's men resumed work on an unfinished water-level battery at Fort Jackson.

Civilians and soldiers alike came to believe that these two forts were impregnable. Major General Mansfield Lovell, the dashing Marylander in command of the Confederate troops in and around New Orleans, had such faith in the forts that, in a letter to Secretary of War Judah Benjamin, he pronounced the Federals' Ship Island build-up "a harmless menace." He assumed that Forts Jackson and St. Philip would force any Federal attack from the south to come by land, and that the broad inland bayous and New Orleans' Chalmette defense line, a string of fortifications four miles south of the city, would easily stop the enemy soldiers.

Most of New Orleans agreed. According to George Cable, the citizens were now confident that the city was unapproachable from the south by land or by river: "Nothing afloat could pass the forts. Nothing that walked could get through our swamps."

The reputation of Forts Jackson and St. Philip was as daunting to the Federals as it was reassuring to the Confederates. As a result, the option of a large-scale land assault on New Orleans from the north dominated Federal strategy.

But logistic problems and the slow start of Federal operations in the West prompted the Navy Department to take a fresh look at the southern approach. Would a naval attack on New Orleans from the Gulf really be as prohibitively costly as the strategists had supposed?

By November of 1861, a plan for a southern assault on New Orleans had been developed under the aegis of Gustavus Vasa Fox, the shrewd and energetic Assistant Secretary of the Navy. Fox had based his plan on a simple but telling observation: Before and during the successful attacks on Hatteras In-

The side-wheeler *Princess,* her steam up, prepares to pull away from the levee at New Orleans in this prewar photograph. Mississippi River trade was at its peak in 1860, when 33 steamship lines served the city.

let and Port Royal, Federal warships had repeatedly steamed within range of the Confederate forts with virtual impunity.

This suggested that shore-based artillery was not nearly as effective as was generally thought, and Fox concluded that a Federal naval force from the Gulf could run upriver past Forts Jackson and St. Philip without suffering serious losses. New Orleans itself had no defense against attack from the river, and once the city came under Federal guns it would have to surrender. Then the two forts, isolated and useless, might well capitulate without a fight.

It was a bold plan that challenged conventional military wisdom. But Fox was convinced that it would work, and his superior, Welles, agreed.

In mid-November, interest in the southern approach was stimulated by the advocacy of Commander David Dixon Porter, the 48-year-old son of a naval hero of the War of 1812. Porter, recently returned from blockade duty on the Mississippi, was stationed in Washington while his ship, the *Powhatan,* was undergoing repairs in the Brooklyn Navy Yard. A tireless self-promoter, he stopped in at the Navy Department to ingratiate himself with Secretary Welles.

Welles was in no hurry to receive Porter, whom he deemed excessively ambitious and "given to exaggeration" about his powers and accomplishments. Yet Porter, by his own account, met two important Republican Senators in Welles's antechamber and took the opportunity to propound a scheme for capturing New Orleans by naval attack from the south. The intrigued Senators thereupon ushered him in to see Welles and urged him to repeat his plan.

Porter proposed that a flotilla of small

sailing vessels, each bearing a mortar, be towed up from the Gulf to bombard the two forts; he said it would take just two days to render the strongholds helpless. Then a fleet of shallow-draft warships would steam past the forts to take New Orleans. Army troops, bringing up the rear, would occupy the forts and the city.

Porter wrote that Welles listened to his plan with interest and suggested that it be brought to the attention of the President at once. Accordingly, the group hurried to the White House. Lincoln, said Porter, immediately embraced the scheme and declared, "This should have been done sooner."

Welles offered a different account of the incident, writing that he had summoned Porter to discuss the existing Navy Department plan to run warships past the forts. Porter, said Welles, "expressed great doubts whether the forts could be passed until reduced or seriously damaged," and suggested that a flotilla of mortar schooners be added to the operation to bombard the forts into submission. Welles conceded that a mortar flotilla would "probably render success more certain," and since President Lincoln was in favor of it, Porter's proposal was adopted as part of the operation.

Whatever the details of its conception, the plan appeared promising. But since it called for the cooperation of the Army, Lincoln felt it was imperative to consult General in Chief McClellan. On the evening of November 15, Lincoln, Welles, Fox and Porter went to McClellan's quarters to discuss their ideas.

McClellan was highly skeptical at first; he said that it would take 50,000 troops to capture New Orleans, and he did not want to part with any of the units he was assembling for his Peninsular Campaign. But he

David Dixon Porter, commander of the Federal mortar flotilla during the advance on New Orleans, delighted in drawing satirical cartoons of his superiors. His peers found him brash. "Porter," claimed a disgruntled fellow officer, "would assassinate the reputation of anyone in his way."

was generally in favor of amphibious operations, as he had recently shown by championing General Burnside's expedition to North Carolina. On learning that a separate army would be raised for the New Orleans expedition, McClellan gave his approval.

The man chosen to raise and lead this new army was the rambunctious Major General Benjamin Franklin Butler. A powerful Massachusetts Democrat who had been won over to the Republican side with the offer of a commission, Butler had quickly become a thorn in the side of the President, McClellan and many others. Those Butler had irritated were eager to see him get the job. Welles dryly remarked: "All would be relieved were

Crewmen of a Federal mortar schooner pose on deck with their keglike, 25,000-pound weapon. During the bombardment of Fort Jackson and St. Philip, downriver from New Orleans, a number of the ship's crew were made ill by the shock of the 13-inch shells being fired at a rate of two per minute.

this restless officer sent to Ship Island or the far Southwest, where his energy, activity and impulsive force might be employed in desultory aquatic and shore duty in concert with the Navy."

Butler would not have overall command of the New Orleans assault: It was to be primarily a Navy operation and required a Navy officer at the top. To fill that crucial role, Welles and Fox selected Captain David Glasgow Farragut, apparently at the suggestion of David Porter.

David Farragut, a vigorous man of 60 who still celebrated his birthday by doing handstands, had devoted his life to the U.S. Navy. At the age of nine he was an acting midshipman on a warship, and while still a boy he had seen combat in the War of 1812 under Porter's father, who raised Farragut as his foster child. During the Mexican War, Farragut made a reputation as a courageous but somewhat radical officer. He authored a daring plan for an amphibious assault on the citadel of Veracruz; though the scheme was turned down, it earned him the admiration of Gideon Welles.

Then came the secession crisis. Although Farragut made his home in Norfolk, he made no secret of his conviction that secession was treason. As Virginia moved toward a break with the Union, he packed his bags and, with his Southern-born wife, moved north to the village of Hastings-on-Hudson near New York City. He offered his services to the government, only to receive a disappointing assignment to the Navy Retirement Board. Farragut performed his work cheerfully, but he longed for a command.

Farragut's appointment to desk duty was clearly influenced by his Southern connections. Gustavus Fox conceded as much; he gave Porter verbal orders to sound out his foster brother's attitude toward the War and the Confederacy — without mentioning a possible attack on New Orleans.

Porter arranged to meet Farragut at the Brooklyn Navy Yard. There they chatted for a while about family matters. Then, as Porter recalled the meeting, he casually mentioned some former colleagues who had chosen to serve the South.

"Those damned fellows will catch it yet!" Farragut remarked with some vehemence.

Encouraged, Porter asked, "Would you accept a command such as no officer in our navy ever held to go and fight those fellows?"

Suddenly Farragut realized that Porter's visit had a serious purpose. He blurted out, "I cannot fight against Norfolk."

Porter deliberately put pressure on this tender spot, declaring, "Then you are not the man I came after, for Norfolk will be the very place to be attacked first, and that den of traitors must be wiped out."

This was a cruel test, for Farragut still had family and friends in Norfolk. But he quickly put sentiment aside and, angered that his

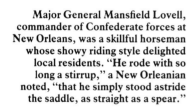

loyalty had been questioned, shouted at Porter, "I will take the command, only don't you trifle with me!"

Within a few days, Farragut received orders to report to Washington. On December 21, he met with Fox at the home of Postmaster General Montgomery Blair and learned, to his delight, that the target was to be New Orleans, not Norfolk. "Mr. Fox then handed him the list of vessels which were being fitted out and asked him if they were enough," wrote Blair. "He replied that he would engage to run by the forts and capture New Orleans with two thirds of the number."

Meanwhile, Porter was busy gathering and equipping his mortar flotilla. The Navy had already purchased 22 ships in New York and Philadelphia — 19 sailing schooners, a supply ship and two smaller sailing vessels. Porter arranged to have twenty 13-inch mortars and 30,000 shells cast in Pittsburgh. He contracted with a New York company for gun carriages that swiveled on tracks, allowing the ponderous mortars to be trained in any direction. Most of the schooners were also armed with two 32-pounders. In addition, Porter obtained seven steamers to tow the schooners into position. Finally, he set about recruiting crews for his vessels and soon signed up a full complement of 700 men and 21 officers.

On January 9, Farragut was officially named flag officer of the West Gulf Blockading Squadron. His flagship was to be the *Hartford*, a three-year-old, 24-gun screw, or propeller-driven, sloop of 2,900 tons, with a draft of just over 17 feet. For the rest of his all-wooden fleet, Farragut would have the big frigate *Colorado*, three additional sloops of the *Hartford's* class, one sailing sloop, the heavy side-wheel sloop *Mississippi*, three lighter sloops and nine gunboats. The fleet — excluding Porter's mortar schooners — mounted 166 guns and 26 howitzers. In Farragut's view, this was more than a match for anything the Confederates might throw at them — excepting the long-rumored ironclads.

On February 20, 1862, Farragut arrived with his fleet at Ship Island. He spent the next four weeks there, awaiting Porter's mortar ships and the bulk of the 18,000 troops that General Benjamin Butler would have at his disposal. The plan of attack called for Butler's troops to sail to the Isle au Breton Sound, put ashore, and march overland to strike the forts from behind.

Finally, all was in readiness. On March 7, Farragut sailed from Ship Island to the lower

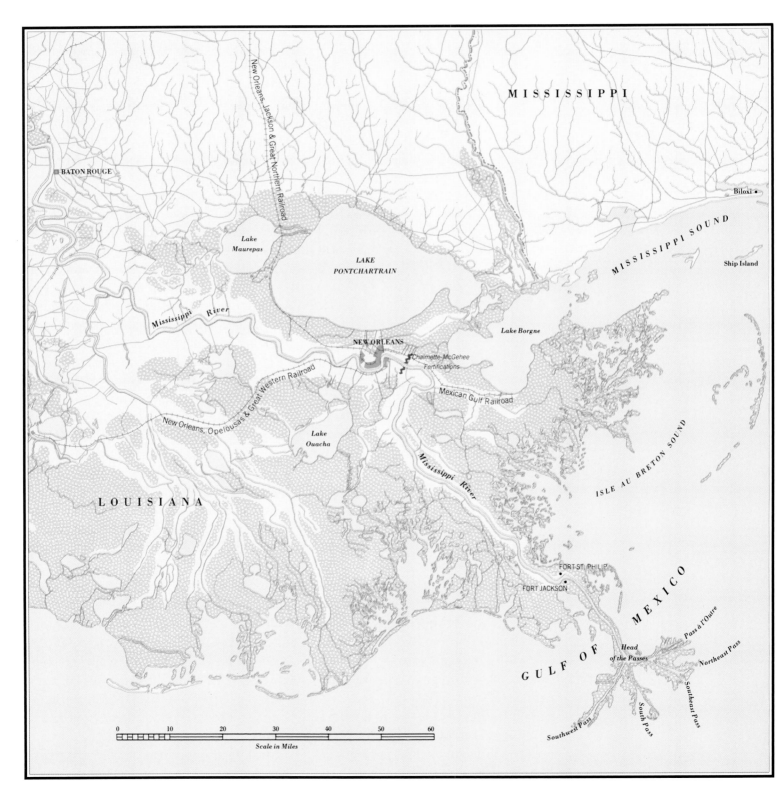

MISSISSIPPI

BATON ROUGE

Biloxi

New Orleans, Jackson & Great Northern Railroad

MISSISSIPPI SOUND

Lake
Maurepas

LAKE
PONTCHARTRAIN

Ship Island

Mississippi   River

Lake Borgne

NEW ORLEANS

Chalmette-McGehee
Fertifications

New Orleans, Opelousas & Great Western Railroad

Mexican Gulf Railroad

Lake
Ouacha

Mississippi River

ISLE AU BRETON SOUND

LOUISIANA

FORT ST. PHILIP

FORT JACKSON

GULF OF MEXICO

Pass à l'Outre

Head
of the Passes

Northeast Pass

Southeast Pass

South Pass

Southwest Pass

0   10   20   30   40   50   60

Scale in Miles

The Federal plan to capture New Orleans called for Flag Officer David Farragut to assemble his fleet on the lower Mississippi and then run his ships past Forts Jackson and St. Philip. As the fleet steamed upriver, troops under Major General Benjamin Butler would then land along Isle au Breton Sound and advance overland to attack the two forts. New Orleans' only remaining defense would be the weak Chalmette-McGehee fortifications four miles below the city.

delta, where the five passes from the Mississippi River splayed out into the Gulf. Now Farragut began the tedious task of maneuvering ships over the bars. Since the blockade had taken effect, the channels, normally maintained by dredging, had become heavily silted through disuse. The smaller ships, including Porter's mortar flotilla, had no difficulty entering the river through Pass à l'Outre, but the larger vessels, sent to the deeper Southwest Pass, faced hard going. Not until April 8 did the big ships finally bull their way across the bar, steaming ahead full speed until the sand stopped them, then backing off to repeat the process. Even then, Farragut's largest vessel, the *Colorado*, which drew 23 feet of water, failed to break through and was left behind. Some of her fighting crew and guns were distributed among the other ships.

As the Federal ships slowly gained access to the main riverway, New Orleans at last acknowledged the peril from the south. On March 15, General Lovell declared martial law, and a week later he informed his superiors in Richmond that an attack on the forts was imminent. If the forts were reduced or bypassed, his only hope lay with the two ironclads. The *Louisiana's* engine had been installed but was not yet working. The *Mississippi* still lacked its 50-foot central drive shaft, which was being cast at a Richmond rolling mill.

At New Orleans the various naval forces in the area assembled to meet the Federal challenge. The ships belonged to three separate commands. One was the River Defense Fleet, a collection of 14 tugs and steamers that cost the Confederate government $1.5 million to make ready for battle. These vessels, piled high with cotton bales to protect their engines, mounted only one or two guns each, but their prows were strengthened with iron and they were meant to be employed primarily as rams. Their tactical use was left to the discretion of their captains, old salts who presumably knew their business so well that they needed no guidance. General Lovell had been ordered by Richmond to send the 14 converted rams upriver to Memphis to guard against the expected Federal attempt to descend the river. Fearing there was greater danger of New Orleans being attacked by river from below, Lovell retained six of the vessels to face that threat.

Also at New Orleans were two converted steamers, the *Governor Moore* and the *General Quitman*, under the command of the Louisiana State Navy — one of several such state flotillas maintained in the Confederacy. The two vessels mounted a total of four guns and had iron-reinforced prows.

The third and potentially most powerful force at hand belonged to the Confederate States Navy. The Navy decided that its ironclad *Louisiana*, though still without motive power, should be towed downriver from Jefferson City and moored above the twin forts to be used as a floating battery. Then there was the *Manassas*, the hulking one-gun ironclad ram that had chased the Federals from the Head of the Passes the previous October. Of the other Confederate Navy ships in the area, only the *McRae*, mounting eight guns, was capable of doing any harm to an enemy flotilla.

Theoretically, Confederate Flag Officer John K. Mitchell was responsible for all three naval forces at New Orleans. But he had no real authority to coordinate their movements. The Louisiana and Confeder-

63

ate Navy captains, like those of the River Defense Fleet, were entirely and worrisomely on their own.

And Farragut's fleet, one of the largest yet assembled under the Stars and Stripes, kept coming on. On April 17, Porter's mortar schooners were towed into position. Two thirds of these ships took up stations by a fringe of trees on the west bank of the river, within striking distance of both forts but hidden by a bend in the river from enemy view; only the tops of their masts showed, and these were camouflaged with tree branches. The rest of Porter's vessels were deployed at intervals across the river. Because Fort Jackson was the stronger of the two bastions and was closer to the barrier the Confederates had laid across the river, the Federals decided to make it the prime target of their bombardment. Farragut's main force paused a mile or so downstream, waiting for the mortars to clear the way.

At about about 9 a.m. on the morning of April 18, Porter's lead mortar ship by the west bank opened fire on Fort Jackson. Then the next ship opened up, and the next, with the firing timed so that a shell arced toward its target every two minutes.

By dusk, more than 1,000 rounds had been lobbed at Fort Jackson. Many of them found their mark, and it seemed that Porter might make good on his boast to reduce the strongpoints in just two days. Fort Jackson's wooden citadel and barracks were ablaze by the end of the day, and General Duncan feared that the magazines were also in danger of igniting. But the defenders huddled inside the brick casemates, and most of the guns remained fully operational. A little after sunset, Porter ordered the firing to cease.

At dawn on the 19th, Porter's vessels opened up with renewed fury on Fort Jackson. More damage was inflicted, particularly on the fort's parapets and platforms. A number of guns were dislodged or disabled, but some of these were quickly put back into working order. Inside the fort the men had suffered from the ceaseless roar of the mortars and the constant fires, but they found to their surprise that their casualties were few. At the end of the second day, the fort remained essentially intact.

In three more days of merciless bombardment, Porter hurled thousands of rounds at the stronghold. With each passing day the Federal fire became less accurate, owing partly to the exhaustion of the gun crews and partly to defective mortar fuses, which caused the shells to explode in midair.

Porter finally gave up trying to time the fuses, and ordered the shells fired so that they would explode on impact or shortly thereafter. Many of these shells embedded themselves deep in the soggy earth and raised cascades of mud when they went off. One round caught a Confederate between the shoulder blades and hammered him deep into a mushy parade ground. Later a shell exploded at the same spot and flung the Confederate corpse high into the air.

By Easter Day, April 20, Farragut was growing impatient. Since the bombardment was having little effect, he decided to run the gantlet of the forts as soon as possible.

That night, two gunboats of Farragut's flotilla, the *Itasca* and the *Pinola,* moved up to the chain barrier. Under cover of darkness, sailors from the vessels slipped onto one of the hulks and set to work to release the chain. An enemy rocket lighted up the river, and Confederate guns at once began to fire on the intruders. But the Federal sailors kept

A contemporary engraving offers a bird's-eye view of the Federal fleet running the gantlet between Fort Jackson (*bottom*) and Fort St. Philip before dawn on April 24, 1862. Earlier in the night, a Federal gunboat had opened the way by cutting a hole in the chain barrier strung across the Mississippi by the Confederates.

up their work until they had severed the chain and opened a great gap in the barrier. Shortly thereafter, the rapid current swept the *Itasca* toward shore and grounded her there. The *Pinola* towed her sister ship back into the stream, and both ships got away downriver with their chain-breakers safely aboard. The barrier on which the Confederates had pinned so much hope was breached.

Still, Farragut waited in deference to Porter. Porter's mortar schooners and the Confederate forts continued their drumfire, with no change in the situation. To Farragut's irritation, Porter, on the 23rd, asked for still more time to reduce the forts. "Look here, David," Farragut replied. "We'll demonstrate the practical value of mortar work." He ordered his signal officer, B. S. Osbon, to climb up the mizzen and observe the effects of the bombardment, waving a red flag for every shell that fell within Fort Jackson and a white flag for every shell that missed its target. Porter and Farragut saw the white pennant unfurled again and again, and the red one only rarely. Farragut had made his point. "There's the score," he said. "I guess we'll go up the river tonight."

Originally, Farragut had planned to have his flagship, the *Hartford*, lead the flotilla; he thought it only right that the commanding officer should put himself and his ship in the position of greatest peril. But his captains dissuaded him, arguing that if the flag officer should be killed or badly wounded as the fleet was just getting under way, the resulting confusion would imperil the whole operation. So Farragut agreed to lead the second of the fleet's three divisions. The first, headed by Captain Theodorus Bailey, consisted of eight vessels, including Bailey's flagship, the gunboat *Cayuga*, and two heavy sloops of war, the *Pensacola* and the *Mississippi*. The second division, led by Farragut's *Hartford*, boasted two other powerful sloops, the *Brooklyn* and the *Richmond*. The third division, made up of two light sloops and four gunboats, was under the direction of Commander Henry H. Bell.

Bailey's task was to concentrate his fire on Fort St. Philip, keeping close to the east bank of the river. Farragut was to bombard Fort Jackson on the west bank, while Bell was to steam to the aid of whichever squadron most needed assistance.

Through the evening of April 23, final preparations were made. Protective chains were lowered to cover the ships' sides and protect the engines and powder magazines. Jacob's ladders were hung over the sides so that ship carpenters could quickly descend to repair shell damage to the hulls. The vessels were smeared with mud to reduce their visibility. Gun crews spread ashes and sand behind their guns to prevent men from slipping in the blood of wounded comrades.

Farragut was taking a calculated gamble. Many of his captains opposed his decision to run the forts, arguing that wooden ships were no match for the solid masonry of the two strongholds. Porter had been especially loud in urging Farragut to wait until the mortar fleet had done its job. But Farragut brushed aside the objections. His mind was made up. To his wife he had confided: "I have now attained what I have been looking for all my life — a flag — and having attained it, all that is necessary to complete the scene is a victory. If I die in the attempt it will be only what every officer has to expect."

Although Farragut knew that some of his subordinates disagreed with his decision, he was unaware of the fact that Porter not only opposed him but had been trying to undermine him in self-serving letters to Assistant Secretary Fox. "Men of his age in a seafaring life are not fit for the command of important

A gunner on the Confederate ram *Governor Moore*, unable to aim properly, fires through his ship's bow into the side of the Federal gunboat *Varuna*. In the collision that followed, the *Varuna* was disabled and soon went down in shallow water near the shore.

enterprises, they lack the vigor of youth," Porter had written Fox. "He talks very much at random at times, and rather underrates the difficulties before him, without fairly comprehending them." And on another occasion: "He is full of zeal and anxiety, but has no administrative qualities, wants stability, and loses too much time in talking." Porter now seemed anxious to dissociate himself from Farragut, hoping perhaps to avoid any onus if the expedition failed.

Farragut had no intention of failing. If all went as he expected, the entire fleet would be out of range of the forts within 90 minutes after the battle began. He assumed that there would be a steep price to pay for success. When one of his officers ventured the guess that the fleet would suffer only about 100 casualties, Farragut replied sadly, "I wish I could think so."

At about 2 a.m. on April 24, Farragut ordered two red lanterns hoisted atop the *Hartford's* mizzen. These lights, burning in the pitch black of a moonless night, were the signal to get under way. The warships moved up slowly in battle order toward the now-breached chain barrier.

By 3:30 a.m. the little gunboat *Cayuga*, leading the way, had steamed past the barrier, unseen by the Confederate lookouts. Next came the *Pensacola*. As she reached the barrier, Confederate sentinels dimly perceived the silhouettes of the enemy ships, and the gunners of Forts Jackson and St. Philip opened fire. The river reverberated with the roar of cannon and the bursting of shells. Soon the night sky and the river were bathed in hectic red light. Confederate rafts, set afire and sent drifting downstream toward the flotilla, shot great gouts of flame 200 feet into the air. Ashore, huge bonfires

blazed up, their leaping flames casting still more lurid light on the Federal fleet to help the gunners at the forts. Through it all, Porter's mortar schooners and steamers kept up their own bombardment of the forts. Wrote one observer, "Imagine all the earthquakes in the world, and all the thunder and lightnings together in a space of two miles, all going off at once." To Farragut, who had climbed his ship's mizzen to view the battle, it seemed "as if the artillery of heaven were playing upon the earth."

The Confederate gunners kept firing back, but with little effect; clouds of gun smoke made accurate fire increasingly difficult. One gun commander took aim at a ship in midstream and pounded away. He had expended much of his ammunition before discovering that he was firing at one of the hulks that supported the chain barrier.

Yet Federal warships did take some hits. As the *Richmond* passed within hailing distance of Fort Jackson, she was raked by Confederate shells. She then reeled across the river and was pummeled by Fort St. Philip's guns. One of the *Richmond's* gunnery officers, lanyard in hand, was decapitated by a shot from the fort. As his torso slumped to the deck, the lock string, still clutched in his hand, discharged his gun.

So far, the motley Confederate fleets had not put in an appearance. The most powerful ship, the nearly finished *Louisiana*, was still anchored safely above the forts; Commander Mitchell, who hoped to have her moving under her own steam very soon, declined Duncan's repeated requests to move her downriver where her guns could be used against the mortar fleet. But the rest of the miscellaneous defending vessels were steaming toward the battle.

Now more of the Federal armada was coming under the guns of the forts. Close behind the first division came Farragut's second, the three sloops of war led by the *Hartford*. Farragut's officers pleaded with him to give up his perch on the mizzen for the relative safety of the deck, and moments after he reluctantly complied a shell smashed the rigging in which he had stood.

As the *Hartford* passed through the barrier, a lookout sighted the Confederate tug *Mosher*, which was pushing a fire raft toward the flagship. The *Hartford* maneuvered to avoid the raft, but ran aground on a mud flat below the guns of Fort St. Philip. Doggedly the little *Mosher* came on, pushing the raft against the ship's hull and holding it there. Flames leaped up the *Hartford's* side as her crew attempted to free her.

For a moment, Farragut seemed to give way to panic. He was heard to say, "My God, is it to end in this way?" But he quickly regained control and shouted to a gun crew surrounded by flames, "Don't flinch from that fire, boys. There's a hotter fire than that for those who don't do their duty. Give that rascally little tug a shot." The flag officer even regained his sense of humor. Seeing Signal Officer Osbon kneeling on the gun deck to unscrew the caps from some shells, Farragut called out to him, "Come, Mr. Osbon, this is not time for prayer."

The crisis soon was over. The gun crew sank the tug with two shots, and the fire raft drifted away. Fire-fighting crews climbed the rigging and doused the flames on the *Hartford's* masts. Then, with a great lurch, the ship pushed off from the mud flat and went back into action.

While the shore batteries and Farragut's ships were exchanging fire, the Confederate

TO THE PEOPLE OF NEW ORLEANS.

Mayoralty of New Orleans,
CITY HALL, April 25th, 1862.

After an obstinate and heroic defence by our troops on the river, there appears to be imminent danger that the insolent enemy will succeed in capturing your city. The forts have not fallen; they have not succumbed even beneath the terrors of a bombardment unparalleled in the history of warfare. Their defenders have done all that becomes men fighting for their homes, their country and their liberty; but in spite of their efforts, the ships of the enemy have been able to avoid them, and now threaten the city. In view of this contingency, I call on you to be calm, to meet the enemy, not with submissiveness nor with indecent alacrity; but if the military authorities are unable longer to defend you, to await with hope and confidence the inevitable moment when the valor of your sons and of your fellow-countrymen will achieve your deliverance. I shall remain among you, to protect you and your property, so far as my power or authority as Chief Magistrate can avail.

JOHN T. MONROE,
MAYOR.

A Northern cartoon mocks Mayor Monroe's reluctance to surrender New Orleans by depicting him as a helpless sea turtle indulging in sham heroics before two Yankee tars. In a letter to Farragut, Monroe had declared: "The city is yours by the power of brutal force and not by any choice or consent of its inhabitants."

gunboats began arriving and challenging the Federals. The first U.S. ship to respond was Bailey's *Cayuga*. Having run the forts and steamed well beyond, the *Cayuga* found her way barred by no less than 11 Confederate vessels. Undeterred, the crew manning the *Cayuga's* 11-inch pivot gun took aim at the *Governor Moore* and scored a hit that sent the side-wheeler in search of an easier foe. The clumsy *Manassas* came at the *Cayuga* with her iron ram, but the swift little gunboat maneuvered out of harm's way.

Just behind the *Cayuga*, the *Oneida* and *Varuna* kept up a barrage at the Confederate ships. Before long, this steady fire persuaded five of the six vessels of the River Defense Fleet to retreat. The *Varuna* moved in pursuit, but in her haste the 10-gun screw steamer outdistanced her sister ships and suddenly found herself isolated upriver. Captain Beverly Kennon of the *Governor Moore* went after her, despite the fact that his ship mounted only two guns. Undetected, the Confederate side-wheeler opened fire at close range.

The crew of the *Varuna* was startled, but replied quickly and surely; soon the deck of the *Governor Moore* was strewn with the dead and wounded. Yet Captain Kennon kept closing in. He came so close to the *Varuna* that only his forecastle gun could bear upon her. That gun hit the *Varuna* with two devastating rounds, killing or wounding 12 crewmen. The *Governor Moore* then rammed the *Varuna*, backed off and rammed her again.

The Federal vessel was doomed. She crawled toward the riverbank, but before she could reach it another Confederate gunboat butted her, and she went down quickly. Fortunately for her crew, the water was shallow there, and most of the men managed to cling to the tops of the protruding masts. In time they were rescued by other Federal ships.

The *Governor Moore*, badly shot up, made for the west bank of the river, pursued by five U.S. warships. Their guns all but obliterated the gallant little steamship. Captain Kennon set her wreckage on fire and then surrendered. Of his 93-man crew, 57 had been killed and 17 wounded.

Another courageous fight was put up by the *Manassas*. Her captain, Lieutenant A. F. Warley, moved on the Federal sloop *Pensacola* after his attempt to ram the *Cayuga* had failed. When the *Pensacola* maneuvered out of the way, Warley rushed at the U.S.S. *Mississippi* and struck her a glancing blow. Then he made for the sloop *Brooklyn* as she cleared the chain barrier. He struck his new target a fearful blow that crushed both the inner and outer planking below the water line. Had it not been for the *Brooklyn's* protective chains, the blow would have been fatal. The *Manassas* then backed off and started upstream, but her weak engines could make little headway against the current. So Warley took the

Ships of Farragut's Fleet

The *Miami,* a side-wheel, schooner-rigged gunboat with both bow and stern rudders, was used to tow mortar schooners.

Two of the mortar schooners that bombarded Forts Jackson and St. Philip lie side by side along the shoreline at Baton Rouge.

The lightly armed *Winona*, one of the so-called 90-day gunboats hastily built after the outbreak of war, lost most of its bow gunners to shellfire from Fort Jackson.

Farragut's flagship, the *Hartford*, was a deep-draft, oceangoing vessel armed with 24 guns.

Manassas downriver, hoping to engage and do mischief to Porter's mortar fleet.

That tactic also failed: Warley ran straight into a barrage from the forts, whose gunners mistook the *Manassas* for a Federal ship. The *Manassas* was again forced to turn about, and this time found herself under the guns of the *Mississippi*, whose crew was eager for revenge. The *Mississippi* came on like a fury, intent on running the *Manassas* down. But Warley dodged the blow and ran his ship ashore; the crew made good their escape as the *Mississippi* riddled the ironclad with sev-

eral broadsides. The *Manassas* soon drifted downstream in flames. As she passed Porter's mortar flotilla, she exploded and sank.

Elsewhere, an ironic fate overtook Lieutenant Thomas B. Huger, captain of the Confederate warship *McRae*. Huger, sighting the Federal gunboat *Iroquois* as she steamed through the gap in the chain barrier, pelted the ship with grapeshot. He knew full well that he was taking on an opponent far more powerful than his *McRae*, for Huger had been serving aboard the *Iroquois* at the outbreak of the War. The formidable *Iro-*

In this fanciful engraving, defiant citizens of New Orleans meet the Federal landing party dispatched by Captain Farragut on April 25, 1862, to demand the surrender of the city. An observer on the riverbank noted that at the sight of the Federals, "the crowd on the levee howled and screamed with rage."

Trailed by a threatening mob in New Orleans, U.S. Navy Captain Theodorus Bailey (*left*) and Lieutenant George H. Perkins walk to City Hall to deliver Farragut's ultimatum. A reporter wrote: "It required the intervention of several citizens to prevent violence being offered to the rash ambassadors."

quois raked the *McRae* with grape and canister. In the exchange, Huger was mortally wounded by his former comrades in arms.

The *Iroquois* was the last ship to pass the forts, and as dawn broke over the Mississippi, Farragut's fleet moved beyond range of enemy guns. The whole naval engagement had taken only two hours. The Federals had lost one ship, the *Varuna,* and had suffered 37 men killed and 147 wounded. The Confederate flotilla was a shambles.

By midday on April 24, Farragut's ships were steaming upriver unchallenged. The flag officer had left behind Porter and his mortar fleet, with orders to demand the surrender of the forts. Should Duncan refuse, Porter was to resume the barrage and, if necessary, cover a siege by Butler's army.

Ever since Porter had opened his bombardment, New Orleans had teetered between panic and hope. When the wind was right,

the citizens could hear the rumble of the distant guns, and there was talk of impending doom. Still, the sturdy resistance of the forts seemed to bear out General Duncan's boast, "We can stand it as long as they can."

By the afternoon of April 24, however, despair had set in. "The startling news was brought us that the forts were passed, and the fleet was approaching the city," a prominent citizen later wrote. "Too bad, after all the *promises* to the contrary! We felt how *cruelly* we have been deceived. How had all the grand speeches, loud huzzahs, nightly drills and magnificent parades, showy flags and splendid music benefitted us?"

The city's remaining defenses were pitiful. Pressed with constant demands from Richmond that he send reinforcements to the north, Lovell now had only 3,000 militiamen at hand, some of them so green that he declared himself "unwilling to put ammunition in their hands." The general closeted himself with Mayor John Monroe and told him that he could not successfully defend the city. If he tried, Lovell explained, Farragut would bombard it. To save lives and property, he meant to evacuate his command.

As news of Lovell's decision spread through New Orleans, rioting erupted. Outraged citizens, intent on depriving the Federals of at least some of the fruits of victory, burned hundreds of bales of cotton and tons of foodstuffs stored on the levees. Molasses oozed out of smashed barrels and flowed down the gutters of the streets. Mobs pillaged without hindrance. An enterprising individual rented a horse and cart and hauled away large quantities of sugar, hams, coffee, tea, butter, beans and canned goods.

The greatest Confederate loss was an official act of destruction. Efforts had been made to tow the unfinished ironclad *Mississippi* upriver, out of the enemy's reach. Those attempts failed, so the leviathan was set afire. Her blazing hulk floated downstream, past the Federal fleet she had been expected to destroy.

By the morning of April 25, the frenzy in New Orleans had yielded to a mood of sullen desperation. Now people gathered in knots, muttering charges of treason while they waited for the Federal ships to appear. Farragut's fleet moved north without haste. Just below the city there remained a final barrier, the weak Chalmette line to the east and the McGehee batteries on the west bank of the river. The Confederate gunners tried to stop the Federals but were quickly silenced.

At 1 p.m., Farragut's fleet arrived at New Orleans. One by one the warships anchored in the river, where they lay, as George Cable put it, "like evil messengers of woe at our very front." Farragut sent Captain Bailey, Lieutenant George Perkins and a guard of sailors ashore under a flag of truce to present his demands to the city's authorities.

The small party docked at the levee, still wreathed with acrid smoke from the previous day's fires. Facing the Federals was an angry crowd. Defiantly the citizens waved Confederate and Louisiana flags and a few pistols. The two Federal officers, leaving their guard behind, climbed on to the levee amid wild shouts of "Hang them!" "Kill them!" "Hurrah for Jeff Davis!" Ignoring the threats, Bailey and Perkins walked stiffly toward City Hall with the crowd dogging their footsteps. Cable, who was shouting taunts along with the others, later said that the officers' walk to the center of town was "one of the bravest deeds I ever saw done."

At City Hall, Bailey met Mayor Monroe and came directly to the point: The city must surrender unconditionally. Monroe replied that New Orleans was under martial law, and therefore he had no authority to surrender; General Lovell, whose militia had evacuated the town, would have to be consulted. In due course, Lovell appeared and declined to surrender New Orleans, but he agreed to withdraw his authority over the city to permit the mayor and his council to make any arrangement they found necessary.

During these discussions, the mob had grown larger and more unruly. Several citizens forced their way into the building and were pounding at the doors of Monroe's chambers, demanding that the Federal officers be turned over for summary justice. Bailey and Perkins were escorted out a rear door and driven back to the levee in a closed carriage, while Lovell and Pierre Soulé, a member of the city council, tried to calm the crowd. Soulé's announcement that Lovell had refused to surrender was loudly cheered, and the general took the occasion to remind the townspeople that he had done his best to defend them against overwhelming odds. Then Lovell mounted his horse and rode to the railroad station, where he boarded the last Confederate train from New Orleans to join his command outside the city.

By the evening of the 25th, a standoff had developed between Farragut and city officials. Mayor Monroe advised his council that the best course would be neither formal surrender nor open resistance. Farragut insisted on surrender and demanded that the Louisiana flag be hauled down at all public buildings. But since the twin forts 75 miles below the city were still in enemy hands and Butler's men could not move on to New Orleans until they fell, he did not press too hard.

Confederate Brigadier General Johnson Duncan salutes as he boards the Federal gunboat *Harriet Lane* to surrender Forts Jackson and St. Philip to Captain Porter, waiting at the top of the gangway. Under the terms granted by Porter, Duncan and his men were paroled and allowed to return to New Orleans.

On the morning of April 26, Farragut dispatched another officer, Lieutenant Albert Kautz, to demand surrender once more. Another mob was waiting on the wharf and refused to permit Kautz and his Marine escort to pass. When the Marines raised their rifles, the rabble pushed women and children forward and shouted, "Shoot, Yankees, shoot!" Kautz had been warned to avoid bloodshed, and he told the Marines to lower their rifles. The impasse was at last resolved with the help of an officer of the City Guard, who was allowed to escort Kautz, a midshipman and a Marine to the mayor's office.

Negotiations between Kautz and Monroe got nowhere. The mayor, backed by the council, stuck to his position that he was not empowered to surrender the city, inviting Farragut to occupy it if he dared. While Kautz was conferring with city officials, a group of Federal sailors mounted the roof of the Mint and raised the U.S. flag. The crowd below jeered, and as the sailors departed, a gambler named William Mumford hauled down the Stars and Stripes. The mob vented its rage and frustrations on the flag, tearing it to ribbons. Mumford was the hero of the hour. But after the city was occupied, he would be hanged for his effrontery by order of its military governor, General Butler.

By April 27, Butler's troops had begun landing along the Gulf to open siege operations, and Confederate morale was rapidly deteriorating. General Duncan dispatched messengers to New Orleans to find out whether the city had surrendered; if it had, there would be little point in continuing the struggle. He tried to buoy his men with a rousing proclamation that praised their sacrifice and urged them to "be vigilant and stand by your guns." But the call fell on deaf ears. That night, the Fort Jackson garrison mutinied. The men turned on their officers, spiked the guns and took potshots at anyone who attempted to hinder them. Half of the garrison fled to the bayous. Among the deserters, Duncan reported with puzzlement, were "many of the very men who had stood last and best to their guns throughout the bombardment."

Believing that the garrison at Fort St. Philip had also mutinied, Duncan was now prepared to yield. To his astonishment, Commander Mitchell of the Confederate fleet suddenly appeared at Fort Jackson and proposed to continue the fight. This officer, who had refused to tow the ironclad *Louisiana* into battle position as Farragut was passing the forts, now had high hopes of getting her engines working at last and turning her guns on Butler's forces, who were moving overland to cut off the forts.

Mitchell's offer was too late by several days. Since the forts were now threatened with a combined land and water attack, Duncan decided to go ahead with the surrender. But in a message to Porter accepting the Federal ultimatum, he warned that he had no control over the vessels still afloat.

Mitchell, still unable to put the *Louisiana* into action yet unwilling to hand her over to the enemy, decided to sacrifice the ironclad. As the surrender documents were about to be signed aboard Porter's ship, the *Louisiana* was set aflame and sent drifting toward Porter's flotilla, her magazines filled with powder.

When Porter received word of the ironclad's approach, he raged at Duncan and accused him of "sharp practice." The general replied, "We do not consider ourselves responsible for anything the naval officers do." And he added bitterly, "Their course has been a remarkable one throughout the bombardment. They have acknowledged no authority except their own, and although I am

commanding officer here I have no power to coerce them."

The surrender documents were signed even as the *Louisiana* continued to drift toward the Federal ships. As if to add a final exclamation point to the staggering Confederate defeat, the great ironclad exploded with a deafening roar before reaching any of the Federal vessels.

Late on the afternoon of April 28, the troops manning Fort Jackson were evacuated and shipped upriver to New Orleans. As a tribute to their valor, Porter allowed the Confederate banner to fly from the fort's battlements until the defenders had passed from sight. The next day evacuation of the garrison at Fort St. Philip began. Butler's army then occupied both bastions. The two Confederate garrisons had lost a total of 11 men killed and 39 wounded. The forts themselves, after a week of pounding, had suffered no irreparable damage. Though wooden buildings were incinerated and the casemates were pocked by Federal fire, a Federal officer said of Fort Jackson when he arrived: "It is as strong today as when the first shell was fired."

On the 29th, General Duncan reached New Orleans and informed the civil authorities of the surrender of the forts. A stunned silence spread over New Orleans. At the same time, cheers rang out aboard the Federal ships in the harbor. Farragut ordered ashore a Marine battalion and a detachment of sailors, backed by two howitzers, to haul down all state and Confederate flags and raise up the Stars and Stripes. The men had a little trouble with the flagstaff on the roof of the City Hall; they were unable to unknot the halyards to lower the flag. So Lieutenant Kautz cut the lines with a swipe of his sword, and Boatswain's Mate George Russell then lowered the banner. A crowd cursed the Marines but made no attempt to prevent them from doing their duty.

On May 1, the Federal army began its occupation. General Butler took control of the city. The battle for New Orleans was over.

The fall of New Orleans had immediate strategic consequences. The Federals now had a major port inside the body of the Confederacy; here they could safely service warships, assemble troops and stockpile supplies for operations along the Gulf Coast and farther up the Mississippi. Indeed, within a week of New Orleans' surrender, Farragut would send Captain Thomas T. Craven reconnoitering upriver, and Baton Rouge would soon fall into Federal hands. A little later, Farragut would cruise farther upriver, beyond the formidable batteries at Port Hudson, again applying the radical military principle he had proved out by running the guns at Forts Jackson and St. Philip: Strongholds may be bypassed and neutralized rather than assaulted in strict succession.

Meanwhile, during Farragut's drive to New Orleans, the Federal forces to the north had made headway. General Grant had won the bloody field at Shiloh, and a joint Army-Navy force under Major General John Pope and Flag Officer Foote had cleared the Confederates out of Island No. 10, a stronghold commanding the big bend of the Mississippi in Tennessee. Though Port Hudson still held, and the cities of Vicksburg and Memphis remained in Confederate hands, the Union forces had overcome great obstacles in their campaign to make the Mississippi a Federal thoroughfare.

A Federal gun crew uses a hoist to load their 15-inch Rodman smoothbore with a 400-pound shot. It took two men to ram the shot home.

Big Guns and Lethal Projectiles

The battles for control of Southern coastal forts were dominated by artillery duels between the most powerful weapons of the Civil War — heavy, large-caliber siege and naval guns with bores 6 to 15 inches in diameter. Like other Civil War artillery, these big guns were of two types: the smoothbore, with its smooth internal barrel surface; and the rifle, with its grooved surface. The spiral grooves caused projectiles to spin as they were fired, giving them greater range and increasing the weapon's accuracy.

The big guns employed a wide range of highly destructive ammunition, such as the massive 11-inch, 121-pound shell at right. Ammunition for the smoothbores was generally spherical, and for the rifled guns, conical.

By the start of the War, the shell appeared to have established its superiority over the old-fashioned cannonball by virtue of its explosive force. But the invention of ironclad vessels revived the use of solid shot, which was better suited to pierce the ships' armor.

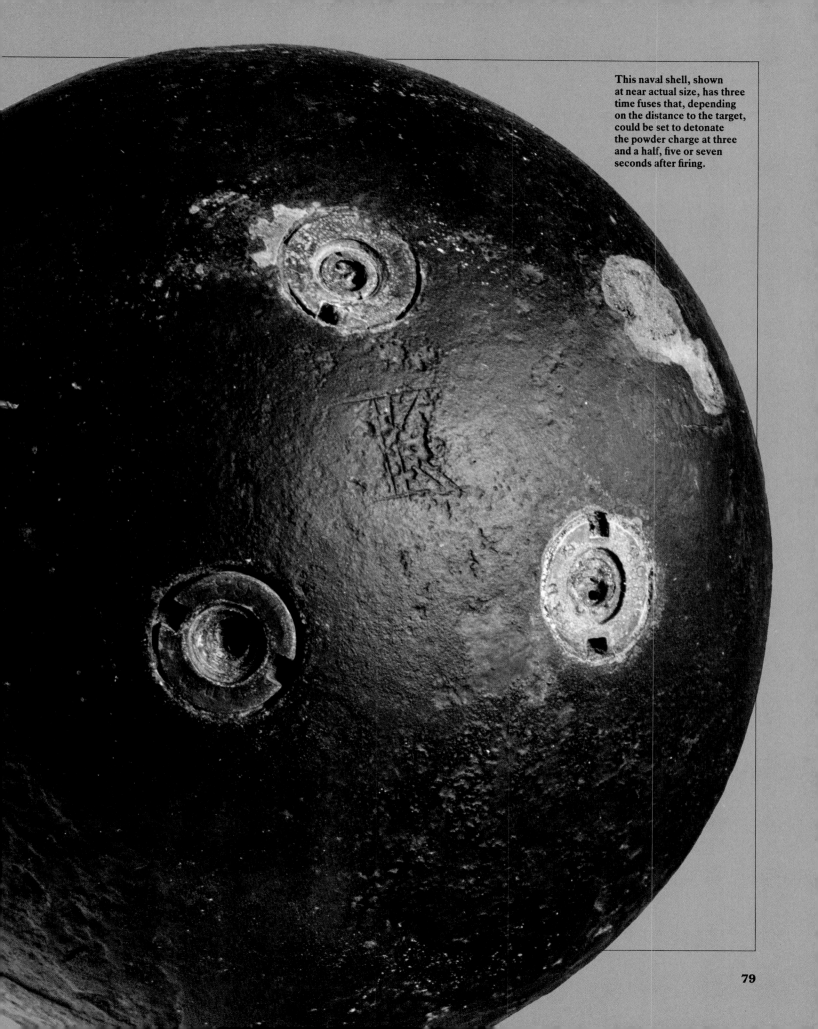

This naval shell, shown at near actual size, has three time fuses that, depending on the distance to the target, could be set to detonate the powder charge at three and a half, five or seven seconds after firing.

The Giant Smoothbores

On the eve of the War, two Federal officers, Thomas J. Rodman of the Army and John A. Dahlgren of the Navy, revolutionized smoothbore cannon by using improved iron-casting techniques to produce a larger and more potent class of gun. Following the principle that the barrel should be thickest where the pressure of combustion is greatest — at the breech — these cannon were bottle-shaped. And they attained truly massive proportions. The barrel alone of a 15-inch Dahlgren weighed more than 10 tons, and one Rodman columbiad fired a shell weighing more than 1,000 pounds. In addition to huge shells *(right)*, the giant smoothbores also could fire grapeshot *(middle)* and canister *(far right)* to defend a battery against infantry or a ship against boarders.

1

2

Federal gun crew drills at a 9-inch Dahlgren smoothbore on the gunboat *Mendota*. The gun's carriage was set on circular tracks so that the crew could slide it into firing position on either side of the deck.

The muzzles of a 15-inch Dahlgren smoothbore and an 8-inch Parrott rifle appear in the turret of the monitor *Passaic*. The smoothbore, too large to fit through the gunport, had to be fitted with a so-called smoke box to keep the muzzle flash and fumes from entering the turret.

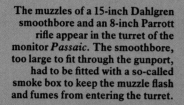

1 SHELL WITH SABOT
This typical smoothbore shell came fitted with a sabot, or wooden band with straps, that prevented an accidental discharge inside the barrel by keeping the fuse pointed outward toward the gun's muzzle.

2 GRAPESHOT
This stand of grapeshot contained nine 4.5-inch iron balls, held in place by a frame. When the device was fired, the frame disintegrated, scattering the shot with deadly effect at ranges exceeding 300 yards.

3 CANISTER
Canister was composed of a sealed tin cylinder containing 48 or more small iron balls packed in sawdust. Upon firing, the cylinder burst, spraying the balls in the pattern of a giant shotgun blast.

Rifling for Accuracy

The Federals' large-caliber rifled guns were designed almost exclusively by Robert P. Parrott, an ordnance engineer. Bolstered by a wrought-iron band shrunk around the breech, these Parrotts had far greater range and accuracy than big smoothbores, yet required much smaller powder charges.

John M. Brooke designed similar guns for the Confederacy. But manufacturing them in the industry-poor South was a problem. To make do, the Confederates ran British rifles, such as the Armstrong (*far right*), through the blockade; they also cut grooves in the barrels of obsolete smoothbores, converting them to rifled guns.

The large-caliber rifles of both sides did have one serious flaw: Because of deficiencies in manufacturing technology, they burst with alarming frequency.

1 JAMES SHELL
When this 7-inch, 84-pound James shell was fired, gases entered the projectile's base, passed through its ribs and expanded a lead sabot into the barrel's rifling, which made the shell rotate.

2 HOTCHKISS SHOT
This 6.4-inch shot, made for a Parrott rifle, consisted of two parts: a bottle-shaped top section containing a rod of armor-piercing iron, and a bottom section that expanded a lead sabot (*missing*) into the rifling, imparting spin.

3 DAHLGREN-TYPE SHOT
Patterned after the Federal Dahlgren shot, this 7-inch missile was made by the Confederates for their Brooke rifles. The cup-shaped lead sabot on its end is indented from the gun's rifling, indicating that the shot has been fired.

An 8-inch Parrott rifle, which fired a 50-pound projectile, serves as the forward pivot gun on the Federal steam frigate *Wabash*. Such rifles were also employed by the Army.

Federals display a British-made 8-inch Armstrong rifle captured from the Confederates at Fort Fisher, near Wilmington, North Carolina, in January of 1865.

4 SCHENKL SHELL
Before it was fired, the bottom of this Federal Schenkl shell was encased in a papier-mâché sabot. The sabots were subject to moisture damage that made them swell and sometimes prevented loading.

5 ARMSTRONG SHELL
This 8-inch Confederate shell, made for Armstrong rifles, has a thin iron cap that crushed on impact, igniting the bursting charge. The brass studs on its sides fitted into the gun's rifling.

Stalemate in the Tidewater

When Major General Ambrose Burnside departed North Carolina in July of 1862, leaving the campaign there in the capable hands of his subordinate, General John G. Foster, the main objective of that campaign had yet to be achieved. Although the Federals had taken New Bern, along with the ports of Plymouth and Washington to the north, the vital rail junction at Goldsboro had been neither captured nor destroyed. The railroad from Wilmington to Richmond was still operating as a massive artery for the flow of food and factory goods from Georgia and the Carolinas to Lee's soldiers in Virginia.

General Foster was left with a force of about 8,000, a number far too small to take and hold Goldsboro. For the moment, he contented himself with strengthening his fortifications while he awaited more men and supplies for a march inland. Between July and December, the Confederates and the Federals continued to stage small raids. But by the end of 1862, with several regiments of Massachusetts volunteers added to his command, Foster was strong enough to go on the offensive against a Confederate army depleted by the demands for reinforcements on the northern Virginia front.

Early in December orders came from Burnside, now commander of the Army of the Potomac and about to launch an offensive at Fredericksburg, for an attack on the railroad near Goldsboro. Foster hoped to sever the line; but, failing that, the attack would at least allow the Federals to destroy large quantities of stored crops along the route of march.

On December 11, 1862, Foster, with 10,000 infantrymen, 640 cavalrymen and 40 field guns, marched out of New Bern and headed west along the Trent River road. The troops were met at Southwest Creek, near the town of Kinston, by an enemy force of about 2,000. The defenders were commanded by Brigadier General Nathan G. "Shanks" Evans, a hero of the Confederate victory at the first Battle of Bull Run. Badly outnumbered, Evans suffered heavy losses and was forced back to the town of Whitehall. There he mounted another defense, but again his ranks were riddled by the Federals, and Evans was compelled to withdraw to the vicinity of Goldsboro.

As Foster's Federals neared Goldsboro, they came within sight of their main target, the 220-yard-long railroad bridge over the Neuse River south of Goldsboro. Its destruction would sever the supply line from Wilmington to Richmond.

Anticipating Foster's intent, the Confederates had posted four North Carolina regiments along the railroad on both sides of the bridge. On December 17, Foster sent the 9th New Jersey and 17th Massachusetts through the woods bordering the tracks. The men advanced cautiously toward the bridge, supported by artillery fire.

Despite the hail of shot and shell from the Confederates, two Federals, Corporal James Green and Private Elias Winans, vol-

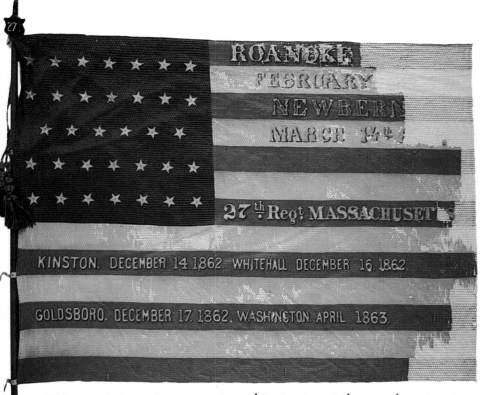

ROANOKE
FEBRUARY
NEWBERN
MARCH 14

27th Regt MASSACHUSETTS

KINSTON. DECEMBER 14. 1862. WHITEHALL. DECEMBER 16. 1862.

GOLDSBORO. DECEMBER 17. 1862. WASHINGTON APRIL 1863.

While campaigning on the coast of North Carolina, the 27th Massachusetts Volunteers inscribed their U.S. flag with the names and dates of six battles in which they fought. All but those at Goldsboro and Washington were clear-cut Federal victories.

unteered to try to set the wooden structure afire with torches. The two men dashed forward, dodging bullets, and made their way to the end of the bridge. There they hurriedly applied the torches, but the wood failed to ignite. Desperate, Private Winans vaulted from the bridge to the riverbank and began grabbing handfuls of twigs, dry leaves — anything that might burn. A bullet passed through his canteen, another tore through his coat, a third creased his face. But he managed to get back to his companion on the bridge, and the two men lit the kindling.

Just as the fire took hold, two comrades arrived on the bridge with more torches. The four pried up a plank and placed a torch beneath it as bullets splintered the wood around them. Then they waited to make sure that the planks would take fire. Finally, as smoke began to creep through the framework of the bridge, the soldiers raced for their own line under cover of Federal infan-

try. The bridge was indeed aflame. General Foster, considering his work to be nearly complete, now ordered his men to tear up several miles of track. This accomplished, he turned his troops around and marched them back to New Bern.

Though Foster termed his expedition "a perfect success," it was at best an equivocal triumph. After six days of marching and fighting, he could claim 739 Confederates killed, wounded or captured, while the Federal toll was 591. And he had captured nine guns, confiscated tons of produce, herded off hundreds of head of livestock and laid waste to many acres of farmland. But the torching of the railroad bridge was a fleeting victory. On December 29, Confederate Major General Gustavus W. Smith, then in overall command of Confederate operations from Richmond to the Cape Fear River, reported to Richmond from Goldsboro that "the bridge is fast being repaired. At present we are subjected to the inconvenience of transshipment across the county bridge, but in a very few days this will be remedied and everything restored to the former condition. I regret that this grand army of invasion did not remain in the interior long enough for us to get at them. As it is, they have utterly failed to take advantage of the temporary and partial interruption of our railroad line."

The Federal troops on Foster's expedition sensed that their 120-mile march had earned them no great glory. As one member of the 5th Rhode Island Heavy Artillery reported, a great deal of energy and blood had gone into the destruction of "fences, houses, cattle, hogs, sweet potatoes and corn."

Still, the loss of livestock and foodstuffs made a deep impression on the Confederates. It was not long after Foster's excursion from New Bern that Robert E. Lee began to devote more attention to the situation on the coasts of Virginia and North Carolina. The Federal advance on Fredericksburg had been thwarted on December 13, 1862, and Lee now felt confident enough about his northern front to dispatch a fourth of his army south of the James River. He had several objectives in mind, chief among them the blocking of any surprise Federal advance on Richmond from the Federal beachheads in Virginia or North Carolina. Lee also hoped to recover the coastal areas lost to the enemy; if that proved impossible, he at least wanted to contain the Federals on the coast. He recognized his dependence on the coastal plain as a source of supply, and he was determined that the region's agricultural bounty should continue to find its way into the warehouses of the Army of Northern Virginia.

To achieve these objectives, Lee created a sprawling new Department of Virginia and North Carolina, and named one of his most able generals, James Longstreet, to head it. About half of Longstreet's command, which he had led so skillfully in the Peninsular and Fredericksburg Campaigns, was detached to serve in the new department. And Daniel Harvey Hill, one of the most competent but contentious Confederate generals, a veteran of the Seven Days and Antietam, was placed in charge of the troops in his native North Carolina.

Like his brother-in-law, Stonewall Jackson, D. H. Hill was a militant Christian with a strong belief in his destiny. But whereas Jackson was secretive, Hill was free with his opinions, a trait that often put him at loggerheads with the bureaucracy in Richmond.

He held Northerners in contempt. As a professor of mathematics and civil engineer-

ing at North Carolina's Davidson College, he had published a series of textbooks that illustrated his regional bias. A mathematical problem in one book began with a swipe at the greed of Northern peddlers: "A Yankee mixes a certain quantity of wooden nutmegs, which cost him one-fourth cent apiece, with a quantity of real nutmegs, worth four cents . . . ." Another problem dealt with two Indiana volunteers at the Battle of Buena Vista who "ran away from the field at the same time."

Hill was in a fighting mood when he took command in North Carolina on February 25, 1863, exhorting his troops "to make the war unpopular with the mercenary vandals of the North." When Longstreet suggested an offensive, Hill champed at the bit. He was eager to drive the Federals from what he called their "rat holes at New Bern and Washington." Longstreet quickly approved an attack to retake New Bern and thus eliminate the threat to Goldsboro.

Around the time that Hill began his advance, Foster's troop strength was reduced. Since his expedition in December, Foster had received substantial reinforcements, but now 10,000 of his Federals were dispatched southward to join the siege of Charleston, South Carolina. Federal and Confederate forces in the New Bern area were roughly equal, with each army consisting of about 15,000 men.

Early in March, Hill gathered his forces at Kinston and began to advance southeast on the Federal stronghold at New Bern. On Friday, March 13, a Confederate reconnaissance force under Brigadier General Junius Daniel came upon Federal pickets some ten miles from New Bern. The Federals fled to their entrenchments at a place called Deep

Gully, where they were attacked by Daniel's men and driven out.

This was a good start, but Hill's offensive soon bogged down, thanks to miscalculations by two of his brigade commanders. A column under Brigadier General James J. Pettigrew had been assigned the crucial task of capturing Fort Anderson, which stood guard over New Bern across the Neuse River from the town. Pettigrew's orders were to surprise the fort, overrun it and turn its guns on any Federal warships coming up the Neuse in aid of the New Bern garrison. Early on the 14th, Pettigrew opened his attack, directing his light artillery in a fierce bombardment of the fort.

After what he deemed an adequate shelling, Pettigrew halted his gunners and sent an officer forward under a flag of truce to demand the surrender of the fort. Its commander, Lieutenant Colonel Hiram Anderson, countered with a ploy. Anderson requested a truce, ostensibly for the purpose of consulting his superior and studying the surrender terms. Pettigrew, against the advice of subordinates, complied. It proved to be a blunder. By the time Pettigrew realized that Anderson was merely stalling, Federal gunboats were moving to the aid of the beleaguered fortress.

Pettigrew drew up his artillery to do battle with the boats. To his dismay, his guns failed to function: One exploded, another would not work at all, and the remaining two merely belched out their shells a few feet. Outwitted and outgunned, Pettigrew retreated.

Failure also dogged a Confederate cavalry brigade under Brigadier General Beverly H. Robertson, who had been assigned to sever the rail line between New Bern and Morehead City, thus blocking reinforcements from the coast. Hill had earlier branded Robertson's unit as "wonderfully inefficient," and its handling of the current task seemed to bear him out. In Hill's words, "Robertson sent me out a lieutenant who partly cut the railroad. He sent out a colonel who saw some Yankees and came back. Robertson did not go himself. We must have a better man." But then, Hill's opinion of all cavalrymen was low: He once offered a reward to anyone who found a corpse with spurs on.

The failures of Robertson and Pettigrew doomed Hill's move on New Bern, and his force soon withdrew. Nonetheless, rumors swept through North Carolina of a great Confederate victory and the recapture of New Bern. One disgusted Confederate wrote home: "You have doubtless read full accounts of the reported recapture of New Bern, and the taking of 1,500 prisoners. The 1,500 prisoners have dwindled down to one cross-eyed Yankee. To the admirers of Daniel H., it would not seem exactly orthodox to say he had no definite object in view when he set out from Kinston; but I must say it looks very like it to a man up a tree."

Hill's next move was against the town of Washington, on the north bank of the Tar

Federal soldiers and former slaves stand among barrels of potatoes and boxes of hardtack outside a quartermaster's depot in occupied New Bern. In the window at lower right, a cook's helper displays loaves of freshly baked bread.

River near its juncture with the broad Pamlico River. Washington was the gateway to one of the most soil-rich regions of North Carolina; its capture would loosen the Federal grip on many square miles of farmland and reopen the area as a source of supply for Lee's army.

Bolstered by 4,000 reinforcements from Wilmington, Hill left Goldsboro in late March and headed north toward Washington through countryside untouched by the War. Some of the troops stopped at a church long enough to sing a hymn. Among them was a soldier of the 32nd North Carolina Regiment, who later wrote: "How strange a contrast — here was a congregation quietly worshiping in their parish church, and passing by was a body of armed soldiers marching to battle!" Hill hoped to catch the enemy unawares and overwhelm the 1,200-man garrison. But the incessant spring rains soon bogged down his marching men and ruined his plans. Learning of Hill's impending attack, General Foster and several members of his staff left New Bern and rushed to Washington to direct its defenses.

By March 30, Hill's force had slogged its way to the outskirts of Washington and was preparing to lay siege to its garrison. To stop enemy reinforcements from New Bern, Hill set up roadblocks and breastworks southwest of town. In order to hold off Federal gunboats, he sited batteries along a stretch of the Tar from Washington to Hill's Point, 6 miles downstream. There he placed obstructions across the river.

Meanwhile, Foster was using his West Point engineering training to advantage. He wrote later, "I caused traverses to be erected along the line of our intrenchments, merlons to be placed on the fort, the door of the maga-

zine to be casemated, the ditches to be enlarged and flooded by means of dams, and the whole garrison generally was steadily kept at work strengthening the defenses; 10,000 rations were put in the fort, with the intention of holding it to the last extremity." Foster had the woods in front of the entrenchments cleared so that enemy infantry approaching the town from the land side would have to traverse half a mile of open ground in the face of artillery and rifle fire. Besides his own artillery, Foster had the support of three gunboats at Washington.

Since Hill was under orders not to risk heavy casualties by storming the town, and Foster lacked the manpower to dislodge the Confederates, the battle for Washington was essentially one of artillery duels. The Confederates sought to limit their artillery fire for fear of running short of ammunition. But each day the 44th Massachusetts' band would mischievously strike up the Southern paean, "Dixie," and the taunt so enraged the besiegers that they stepped up their barrage, forcing the defenders to take cover. For their part, the Federal gunboats would regularly precede the bombardment of Confederate positions with a short calliope concert. After one of these assaults, a Confederate soldier wrote: "They never did any real harm; it was almost as if it were done for an evening's entertainment."

In time, conditions for those on both sides grew difficult. The mud and rain made the Confederates miserable, and the Federals were rapidly running out of supplies and food. One Federal complained to his diary, "We have come down to very small rations of pork and bread, and no beef; and limited to half a dipper of coffee at a meal, while the work is increasing, and hard work, too."

Hill, meanwhile, was accomplishing a vital objective. So long as the Federal garrison remained pinned down at Washington, the Confederates were free to gather food supplies in the area and ship them north on the railroad. Twice, the main Federal force at New Bern tried to relieve Washington. The first attempt came by water. Transports carrying 2,500 men under Brigadier General Henry Prince steamed to the mouth of the Pamlico. But as soon as Prince spotted the Confederate gun emplacements at Hill's Point, he concluded that his chances were none too good, and beat an inglorious retreat. A second effort came overland, led by Brigadier General Francis B. Spinola, a political appointee who knew nothing of warfare. He marched out of New Bern with a brigade and, on encountering a Confederate force at Blount's Creek on April 9, turned tail and fled. In despair, Foster decided that if Washington was to be relieved, he would have to escape from the town and lead a column back from New Bern himself.

Foster got the opportunity he needed on April 13, when the Federal steam transport *Escort*, protective hay bales stacked around her decks, braved the enemy guns along the Tar to relieve Washington. This day the Confederate aim was incredibly poor; the batteries fired 60 rounds at the *Escort* — and missed her every time. The *Escort* brought food, ammunition and reinforcements in the form of the 5th Rhode Island Volunteers.

Two days later, Foster left Washington aboard the vessel. This time the ship was less lucky as it ran the gantlet: It was struck 40 times, but not put out of commission.

During the harrowing trip down the Tar, Foster stood in the wheelhouse, revolver aimed at the pilot, a man named Padrick, who was rumored to be a Confederate sympathizer just looking for an opportunity to ground the vessel under Hill's guns. But the pilot's behavior proved exemplary. Foster recalled that as they were passing the last obstruction in the river, Padrick told him: "I reckon we're all right now." A moment later the pilot was hit. "I'm killed, General," he exclaimed, "but by God, I'll get you through!" He was indeed mortally wounded, but the vessel steamed safely on.

Even as Foster was making his dangerous escape, General Hill began to withdraw. The move was precipitated by a message from Longstreet, who was mounting a demonstration at Suffolk, Virginia. Longstreet needed some of Hill's troops to pin down the Federals there and allow the Confederates to forage in the region. But there were other good reasons for Hill to pull out. The arrival of the *Escort*, and in her wake, two more vessels, had given the besieged Federals enough ammunition and supplies to hold out for several weeks. Hill also faced the increasing risk of an attack from New Bern. Besides, the two-week siege had allowed the Confederates time to complete their foraging in the surrounding countryside. Many of the Confederate soldiers were keenly disappointed at the withdrawal, but one, at least, took a philosophical attitude. He left behind a note that read: "Yankees, we leave you, not because we cannot take Washington, but because it is not worth taking; and besides, the climate is not agreeable. A man should be amphibious to inhabit it."

General Hill vented some of his own frustrations in an official document, his General Order No. 8, thanking his troops but castigating North Carolina militia units that had failed to come to his support. In phrases

Major General Daniel Harvey Hill jeopardized his reputation for hard fighting with his poorly coordinated attack on New Bern in March 1863. After the assault was repulsed by the Federals, one of Hill's men groused: "These big generals don't always have such deep-laid plans as people give them credit for."

laced with sarcasm, he described the state militia's "noble regiments" as consisting of "three field officers, four staff officers, ten captains, thirty lieutenants, and one private with a misery in his bowels." Shortly thereafter, Hill was recalled to defend Richmond during the Gettysburg Campaign.

Not until early in 1864 did Robert E. Lee mount another major effort to retake coastal North Carolina, where the situation was deteriorating for the Confederates. The Federals, unable to extend their coastal domain yet determined to deny enemy troops the fruit of the land, had been conducting devastating raids, destroying crops and livestock, even burning whole towns.

On a foray through the hamlets of Trenton and Pollocksville, for example, the Federals,

according to a Confederate soldier, had left "many fine dwellings mostly all destroyed, having knocked to pieces those which they could not burn — chairs, sofas, bedsteads and all sorts of furniture are broken up and scattered over the streets and fields." At one farm, the Confederate wrote, the Yankees had burned the kitchen, then "killed all the stock on the farm, and the house and yard were full of buzzards."

The raids weakened the morale of the people and helped keep Lee's soldiers hungry. A Connecticut soldier summarized the effect in a letter home, noting that "this whole country, for purposes of maintenance for man or beast for the next twelve months, is a desert as hopeless as the Sahara itself."

Eager to drive out the occupiers, Lee decided to take advantage of the winter lull on the main front in Virginia to send more troops to North Carolina. "I can now spare the troops," he wrote to President Davis on January 2, 1864, "which will not be the case as spring approaches." On this occasion, Confederate troops would be supported by a small Navy fleet. Four ship's boats were sent by rail from Petersburg, Virginia, to Kinston, North Carolina; other boats were shipped from Wilmington and Charleston, and all were launched on the upper Neuse. Commander John Taylor Wood led the flotilla. Again the objective was New Bern.

Lee selected Major General George E. Pickett to command the ground force in this assault. In late January, Pickett set out from Kinston with about 4,500 men, his infantry supplemented by eight rifled artillery pieces, six Napoleon guns and 600 cavalrymen.

The success of the operation depended on close coordination between Pickett's army and the flotilla. Pickett's men were to launch

a three-pronged attack on New Bern on February 1. One column would move on the town from the northwest; a second was to make a wide circle and approach New Bern from the south, along the Neuse River, crossing the railroad bridge over the Trent River to enter the town; a third contingent would capture Fort Anderson, across the Neuse from New Bern, to keep it from shelling the attackers. The men aboard the ship's boats were to seize the three Federal gunboats thought to be patrolling the Neuse.

The offensive went awry from the start. Before dawn on February 1, Brigadier General Robert F. Hoke sent the 31st North Carolina Regiment against a key Federal stronghold blocking the western approach to New Bern at Batchelder's Creek, some eight miles from the town. Hoke expected to surprise the Federals holding the bridge over

the creek, but alert Union pickets sounded the alarm. Before the 31st could reach the bridge, the span had been destroyed. But the Confederates managed to bridge the stream with logs and rout the Federals from their defenses on the opposite bank.

Hoke then led his men to the outskirts of New Bern. He brought the column to a halt and waited to hear the sound of guns from the south, signaling that the second Confederate column, under Brigadier General Seth Barton, was launching its attack on the city from across the Trent River. Barton, however, had suffered a failure of nerve. His scouts' report convinced him that the Federal fortifications on the Trent were too strong to be swept aside, and he dispatched couriers to Pickett, who was with Hoke in front of New Bern, asking for new instructions. Pickett ordered Barton to join him.

Confederate artillerists and riflemen on the banks of the Tar River rake the Federal transport *Escort* as she prepares to negotiate a barrier of wooden piles below Washington on April 15, 1863. One of the shells hit the pilothouse, "scattering the splinters about us promiscuously," recalled the captain.

In 1862, the Federals seized three towns — Plymouth, Washington and New Bern — that commanded access to North Carolina's strategic rivers. From these footholds they attempted raids on the Wilmington Weldon Railroad, a vital supply route for Lee's army in Virginia. The Confederates briefly reoccupied Plymouth and Washington in 1864 but failed in their attempts to dislodge the Federals from New Bern

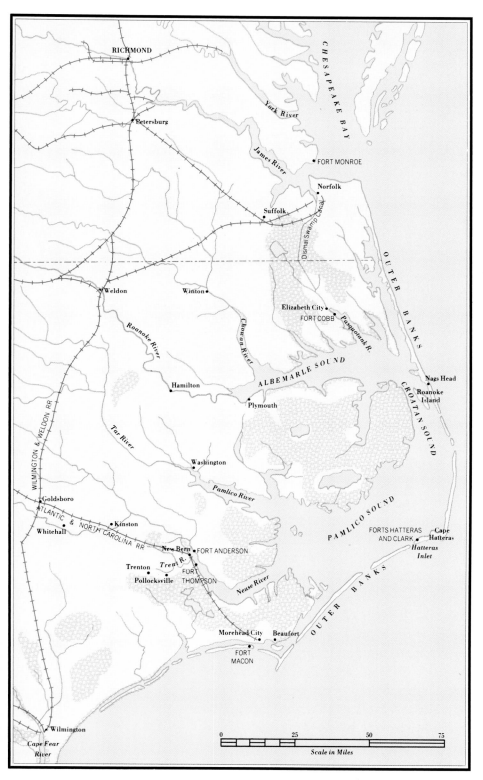

At about this time, Pickett also heard from his third column, under Colonel James Dearing, who was to attack Fort Anderson. Like Barton, Dearing was reluctant to press on. He decided that the fort was too formidable and decided to forgo the assault. With two of his three columns unable or unwilling to attack, Pickett had no choice but to call off the offensive and withdraw.

The Confederate Navy emerged from the aborted offensive with some glory. The flotilla of tiny ship's boats, manned by a force of 35 officers, 25 Marines and 250 seamen, had made the 60-mile journey down the meandering Neuse without incident. Expecting to find three gunboats at New Bern, Commander Wood was sorely disappointed to discover that only one was on duty. But it was a formidable opponent: the four-gun side-wheeler *Underwriter*, the largest Federal ship near New Bern. At 2:30 a.m., under cover of darkness, Wood's fleet approached the *Underwriter*. The Confederate boarders wore white arm bands to distinguish them from the enemy. One officer who took part in the attack recalled: "As I stood up and watched the line, it looked like a naval funeral procession. Not a sound could be heard save the dipping of the oars. Every ear was wide open for the first sound of alarm."

The Confederates were alongside the *Underwriter* before they were spotted. In a moment all was pandemonium as the call to quarters sounded and bluejackets, awakened from sleep, rushed to their battle stations. The Confederate boats closed and snagged the enemy vessel with grapnels. The first Confederate aboard was shot dead, but his mates rushed over him with a yell. One of them wrote: "No one faltered or fell back. The cracking of arms and the rattle of cut-

lasses made a deafening din. The enemy gave way slowly. They fell back under the hurricane deck before the steady attack of our men." After a fierce and bloody exchange, the *Underwriter* was surrendered.

Soon Federal gunners on the nearby shore realized that the ship was in Confederate hands and opened fire. Unable to get up sufficient steam to flee with his prize, Commander Wood set her afire, and he and his men escaped upstream in their small boats. Their feat drew gratifying praise. Confederate Secretary of the Navy Stephen Mallory, for one, hailed the boarding and destruction of the *Underwriter* as a "brilliant exploit."

The failure of the Confederate land force at New Bern prompted General Braxton Bragg, chief military adviser to President

Davis, to call for a switch in leadership. General Pickett was allowed to remain in overall command of the Department of Virginia and North Carolina. But Bragg entrusted the next operation to Robert Hoke, the only Confederate commander who had performed well at New Bern. Hoke was a native of North Carolina, only 26 years old and eager to build a reputation. At Bragg's direction, he began planning a new attack on the Federals, this time on the town of Plymouth, at the mouth of the Roanoke River.

A strategic supply depot, Plymouth was strongly fortified, with a garrison of 2,834 men commanded by Brigadier General Henry Walton Wessells. The land approaches to the town were blocked by a cordon of breastworks, redoubts and obstructions. The harbor, facing north, was guarded by

Officers and sailors line the decks of the U.S. Navy gunboat *Hunchback*, a former Staten Island ferry armed with four Dahlgren guns: a 6-pounder rifle and 12-pounder boat howitzer (*top*), and two 9-inch smoothbores (*bottom*). During the Confederate attack in March 1863 on Fort Anderson, across from New Bern, fire from the *Hunchback* and three other gunboats on the Neuse drove the enemy batteries from the field.

two gunboats, the *Southfield* and the *Miami*, as well as two smaller vessels, all under U.S. Navy Commander Charles W. Flusser.

Despite its impressive defenses, Plymouth was an attractive target for Hoke. Not only would his attacking force outnumber the garrison by about 3 to 1, but he would have a formidable ally in the ironclad ram *Albemarle*, docked a mere 30 miles up the Roanoke River at Hamilton. This ship had been built in a cornfield above Hamilton and had yet to see action. Plated with recycled rails and other scraps of metal smelted at Richmond and Wilmington, the vessel had been well over a year in the making. Even now it was not quite ready for its maiden battle, but the *Albemarle's* captain, Commander James W. Cooke, had orders to join Hoke in capturing Plymouth. The *Albemarle* could confidently take on any wooden ship the U.S. Navy might throw at her. And there was no fear of her facing a Federal ironclad, since they were all concentrated off South Carolina for the siege of Charleston.

The plan called for the *Albemarle* to reach Plymouth on April 18 and clear the town of its river defenses while Hoke's infantry invested the garrison by land. Hoke and his men started out from the New Bern area and on the 17th had Plymouth under attack. By nightfall on the 18th, Hoke's brigade had captured one of the Federals' key strongpoints. To their dismay, however, the *Albemarle* was nowhere in sight. The ram had left Hamilton in ample time, but her engines had failed and her rudder head had broken off. Although repairs were made by workmen who were on board to put the finishing touches on the ironclad, sunken obstructions placed in the river by the Federals caused a further delay. Not until 2:30 a.m. on April 19 did the river rise enough to permit the ram safe passage.

Soon after, the *Albemarle* passed Fort Grey, an outpost of the Plymouth defenses, without replying to its guns. Far bigger quarry awaited the ship; out of the darkness loomed the *Miami* and the *Southfield*. Chains had been strung between the two ships in hopes of catching the ram between them and pounding her into submission with their combined fire. Instead, the *Albemarle* went full steam ahead at the *Southfield* and buried her 18-foot submerged beak deep into the Federal gunboat.

As the *Southfield* went down, the *Albemarle* extricated herself, then went after the *Miami*. The two vessels fought at such close quarters that a shell fired from the *Miami* rebounded off the tough hide of the *Albemarle* and landed back on the *Miami's* deck, where it killed Commander Flusser. The U.S. Navy gunboat then turned tail and fled downriver. Commander Cooke did not follow; he had cleared Plymouth's waterways of enemy ships, and now awaited further communications from General Hoke, whose land forces had resumed their attack as the *Albemarle* approached. In a carefully coordinated assault on the town from the east, south and west, Hoke's men soon routed the Federals and on the morning of the 20th entered Plymouth. General Wessells and his remaining forces were penned up in Fort Williams, an enclosed work in the center of the defenses. Hoke demanded surrender, and Wessells, after first refusing, was quickly forced to comply.

As Wessells later explained in his official report, the Confederate fire was so intense that his men were unable to stand at their guns. "This condition of affairs could not be

long endured without reckless sacrifice of life," wrote Wessells. "No relief could be expected, and in compliance with the earnest desire of every officer, I consented to hoist a white flag and at 10 a.m. of April 20 I had the mortification of surrendering my post to the enemy with all it contained." The haul, according to a report in a Richmond newspaper, included some 2,500 men, 28 artillery pieces, 500 horses, 5,000 stands of small arms, and masses of ammunition.

For this first substantial defeat of the Federals in North Carolina, Hoke was raised to the rank of major general by President Davis. The young lion had hardly received congratulations before he was moving on the Federals at nearby Washington. But when he arrived to lay siege to the town on April 27, he found that its garrison was already being evacuated. As had happened before in this coastal campaign, the major theater in

Virginia had taken priority. This time General Ulysses S. Grant had ordered the troops north to join the Army of the Potomac near a place called the Wilderness.

On April 30, the last Federal troops in the town took ship, leaving behind a shambles of looted and burned-out buildings. The final detachments to depart set fires that quickly spread, consuming half of Washington.

Outraged by this vandalism — which even the U.S. Army considered serious enough to warrant a court of inquiry — Hoke was determined to drive the Federals from their last major bastion on mainland North Carolina, New Bern. For this, the third Confederate attack on the town, he would again require the cooperation of the Confederate Navy in the form of Commander Cooke and the *Albemarle*. Cooke gamely agreed to the undertaking, although he would now be facing not two Federal gunboats but a whole fleet. Furthermore, he would be vulnerable to attack all along the water route as he crossed the Albemarle, Croatan and Pamlico Sounds and ascended the Neuse River to New Bern.

As it turned out, he got no farther than the head of Albemarle Sound. There, on the afternoon of May 5, he found seven wooden gunboats awaiting him: four double-enders (side-wheelers able to steam in either direction) and three smaller vessels. The *Albemarle* held her own in this lopsided battle. The Federal guns were all but useless against her. Even hundred-pound solid shot merely glanced off her sloping iron sides. Not until one of the double-enders, the U.S.S. *Sassacus*, made a run at the *Albemarle* and rammed her at top speed did the ironclad suffer damage and begin to ship water. The *Sassacus*, her timbers split and strained from the collision, stuck fast. The ironclad seized the opportunity to send a cannon shot through her starboard boiler. Escaping steam filled the ship, and the screams of scalded sailors rose above the din of battle.

The two vessels eventually separated, and the crippled *Sassacus* drifted with the current. But the *Albemarle* was in no condition to continue the fight. Her steering mechanism damaged and her smokestack riddled with holes, she was barely able to make her way back to Plymouth. There she lay anchored for almost six months while repairs were being made.

The prospect of having to fight the *Albemarle* again was such a threat that the Federals determined to sink her. On a dark night in October, a small naval detachment under Lieutenant William B. Cushing stole up the river in a launch and exploded a torpedo under her hull. The ram sank to the river bottom, and with her sank the Confederate hopes of loosening the enemy stranglehold on the North Carolina coast.

Even without the *Albemarle*, General Hoke had gone ahead with his assault on New Bern. His forces had reached the town and were experiencing significant successes in preliminary skirmishes on its outskirts when, to his chagrin, he received a message from General P.G.T. Beauregard, the commander at Petersburg, Virginia. Beauregard ordered Hoke to "repair to Petersburg, no matter how far the operations might have advanced." While Lee was engaged with Grant north of Richmond, a Federal army had come up the James River for an attack on Petersburg, and Beauregard was frantically trying to collect troops to meet the threat. Hoke and his men had to depart North Carolina, leaving the towns of Plymouth and Washington virtually undefended. Plymouth again fell to the Federals on October 31, 1864, and Washington soon after.

Yet now, as before, the Union forces could gain little else on the coast of North Carolina. The Federal government simply could not spare enough troops to take and hold their most important objective, Goldsboro. The Federals had to content themselves once again with raiding, confiscating crops and livestock, and burning villages.

After years of campaigning, nothing much had been accomplished. What General Burnside originally envisioned as a quick, surgical operation to cut Lee's supply line had deteriorated into a desultory stalemate.

It was not until March 1865, just a few weeks before Lee's surrender at Appomattox, that Goldsboro — and the railroad to Richmond — finally fell.

Portfolio of the Siege Years

For nearly four years, Charleston, South Carolina, birthplace of secession and spiritual capital of the South, stood defiant in the face of a relentless Federal siege from the sea. From August 1863 onward, the city that Northerners knew as the Cradle of Rebellion was rocked by exploding shells from ironclad warships and siege guns emplaced on captured islands nearby. "The thunder of artillery," claimed an observer, "was as familiar as the noises of passing vehicles in more fortunate cities."

The brunt of the Federal fire was directed at Fort Sumter (*left*), the anchor of the harbor defenses. In 280 days of almost nonstop bombardment, Federal guns fired about 46,000 rounds at the three-tiered citadel, reducing it to rubble and killing 56 men and wounding 267.

To document Charleston's heroic resistance, General Pierre G. T. Beauregard asked Conrad Wise Chapman, a 22-year-old soldier-artist with the 59th Virginia Volunteers, to illustrate the siege. For months, Chapman clambered about the Confederate fortifications with his sketchbook, pencils and brushes. A soldier recalled the artist's bravery: "Often he sat under a heavy cannonade. He minded it no more than if he had been listening to the post band."

In March 1864, Chapman was granted a furlough to travel to Italy, where his father, the distinguished Virginia-born painter John Gadsby Chapman, had his studio. There Conrad Chapman developed his sketches into a series of oil paintings, several of which appear on these pages.

A tattered Confederate flag whips in the wind above a lookout on Fort Sumter's shell-battered parapet in this painting by Conrad Chapman. In the distance, beyond Cumming's Point on Morris Island, Federal ships blockade the harbor entrance.

On the south side of Charleston Harbor, Confederate gun crews manning Battery Simkins on James Island duel with Federal artillery on Morris Island, a mile away

Federal work parties swarm over Cumming's Point on Morris Island as a Federal warship — its smokestack visible behind the dunes — stands by. Chapman, wh

sketched the scene looking through a telescope from Charleston, noted that whenever a shell burst over Cumming's Point, "the Yankees would disappear as by magic."

A sentry stands ramrod straight on a rampart at the Laurens Street battery in Charleston. Near the entrance to the battery's magazine at right is a row of caniste

harges. In the harbor, a Confederate ironclad steams toward Castle Pinckney; on the horizon are Fort Sumter *(center)* and Sullivan's Island *(left)*.

Inside the desolate, flooded ruins of Fort Sumter, Confederate soldiers huddle around campfires on a chill dawn in December 1864. By this time the beleaguere

106

efenders had to work constantly, wrote Chapman, "getting ready sandbags for breaks in the fortifications."

As the setting sun lights Charleston's spires, Confederate soldiers lower the flag at Fort Sumter. John Gadsby Chapman finished this painting from his son's sketc

Charleston under the Gun

"A desperate stand will be made at Charleston, and their defenses are formidable. Delay has given them time and warning, and they have improved them. They know also that there is no city so culpable, or against which there is such intense animosity."

GIDEON WELLES, U.S. SECRETARY OF THE NAVY

In the spring of 1862, the capture of Charleston, South Carolina, was high on the list of Federal priorities. Even though the U.S. Navy controlled the Atlantic seaboard from the Potomac River to Key West, its efforts to blockade Charleston Harbor had proved less than a perfect success. There, day after day, swift, low-hulled blockade runners took full advantage of the harbor's complexities — its three approach channels, its shifting shoals and tricky currents — to defy the Federal patrols and slip into port, bringing precious cargoes of supplies that helped the Confederacy to keep fighting. The only sure way to close this supply line from abroad was to capture the city itself.

The Federals had another, more visceral reason for targeting the city — revenge. Charleston Harbor was the site of Fort Sumter, where the first shots of the War had been fired, tearing the Union asunder, and Northerners hated the city as they did no other. As a U.S. Navy officer put it: "The desire was general to punish that city by all the rigors of war."

Charleston also played on Southern emotions. To Confederates, the city was a symbol of freedom from Federal tyranny, one they were prepared to defend to their last breath. Thus, from the very beginning, Charleston was destined to be a bloody battlefield, the scene of a prolonged and bitter struggle in which both sides would expend prodigious amounts of energy.

The capture of Port Royal, South Carolina, in November 1861 gave the Federals an excellent staging area for an advance on Charleston. In the spring of 1862, Brigadier General Henry W. Benham, a divisional commander at Hilton Head Island, drew up a plan that looked good on paper. Benham proposed landing a force on the lower end of James Island (*map, page 113*), south of Charleston. Under cover of Navy gunboats, the troops would rapidly advance north across the island, overwhelming the defenders before they could be reinforced. The attackers would then dig in near Charleston Harbor, beyond the range of Fort Sumter's guns but within easy shelling distance of the city. Placed under siege, Charleston would surely surrender.

Benham's superior, Major General David Hunter, gave the go-ahead that spring, after the Navy assured him that their gunboats had possession of the Stono River, gateway to James Island. When the expedition got under way in early June, the Northern press hailed it with great fanfare. "Doom hangs over wicked Charleston," prophesied the New York *Tribune*. "If there is any city deserving of holocaustic infamy, it is Charleston." But a signal failure of generalship was soon to quash Northern hopes.

When Confederate Major General John C. Pemberton, the commander of the Department of South Carolina, Georgia and Florida, got word that Federal ships were gather-

Powerful seacoast guns, dug into the White Point Gardens at the foot of the East Battery in Charleston, point toward the harbor entrance. These emplacements, along with Fort Sumter and the harbor's other strongpoints, made Charleston the most formidable coastal city in the Confederacy.

ing at Stono Inlet, he rushed every available man to James Island. There, Brigadier General Nathan "Shanks" Evans hastily set the troops to work building a strong earthwork south of Secessionville, a hamlet of summer cottages belonging to James Island planters. Blocking the attackers' path, the breastwork lay across a long, narrow cotton field only 125 yards wide and bordered on both sides by impassable marshes.

By the time Benham's troops arrived, they faced about 500 entrenched Confederates under Colonel T. G. Lamar, who had seven artillery pieces at his command. Benham had reportedly been ordered by Hunter not to attack until reinforced, but he forged ahead. At first light on June 16, the Federals were in motion, supported by artillery fire from gunboats on the Stono River. For some reason, Benham ordered the charge to be made by a brigade in line of battle, even though the area between the marshes was scarcely wide enough for a regiment. As a result, the men had to press together to avoid the marshland, and the battle line became a tangled mess. While the confused regiments were struggling to form up, the center of their line was blown apart by Confederate grapeshot. Still, the charge went forward, into what one Federal officer described as a "per-

fect storm of grape, canister, nails, broken glass and pieces of chain which swept every foot of ground."

The first wave of attackers was shattered. When the 46th New York in the second brigade tried to advance, part of its line was swept backward by remnants of the retreating 7th Connecticut and 28th Massachusetts. Even worse, shells from the gunboats a mile away began to land short, among the charging Federals. Adding to their problems, 2,000 fresh Confederate troops — South Carolina infantrymen — had just arrived to aid the defenders.

Yet the Federals pressed forward, and after half an hour of bloody fighting some of them had reached the Confederate works and were grappling hand to hand with the defenders. A fresh Federal division was lined up to provide the extra push. But, with victory seemingly within his grasp, Benham suddenly ordered a retreat, leaving behind 683 dead, wounded and missing. The 8th Michigan, vanguard of the assault, had lost one third of its men, including 13 out of 22 officers. Thus ended the Battle of Secessionville, called by one Federal soldier "the culmination of obstinacy and folly." For this fiasco, Benham was placed under arrest, sent North and demoted.

The U.S. Navy, meanwhile, was busy working up its own plans for taking Charleston. The ability of the *Monitor* to withstand punishment in her duel with the more heavily armed *Merrimac* at Hampton Roads on March 9, 1862, had convinced Secretary of the Navy Gideon Welles and his assistant, Gustavus Fox, that the revolutionary little ironclad was just the weapon to bring Charleston to her knees. Lobbying before a Congressional committee for an entire fleet of such ships, Fox rashly asserted that the *Monitor* was impregnable, and could steam into Charleston Harbor all by herself. It would be a simple matter, Fox contended, for a flotilla of monitors to compel a quick surrender. He was determined that the Navy should have the glory of capturing Charleston, and the sooner the better. As Fox put it, he had two responsibilities: "First to beat our Southern friends; second to beat the Army."

In Fox's plan for the Charleston operation, the Army would play only a secondary role: Ten thousand soldiers would be landed on the undefended shores of Folly Island, south of the city, and stand by to occupy Charleston once it had been battered into submission by the Navy's guns. It would be another New Orleans.

But unlike New Orleans, which had been defended by two strongpoints downriver, Charleston Harbor was, in the words of a U.S. Navy officer, "a cul-de-sac, a circle of fire" comparable to "a porcupine's quills turned outside in." The imposing ring of forts that protected it would have to be silenced; otherwise, they would pound the fleet as it sailed through the harbor.

During the summer of 1862, as construction of Fox's fleet of monitors proceeded in the North, the Confederates busily went about strengthening Charleston's defenses. When South Carolina Governor Francis W. Pickens complained to Jefferson Davis that General Pemberton was not the best man for the job, Davis replaced Pemberton with General Pierre Gustave Toutant Beauregard. Charlestonians were exultant; Beauregard was one of their heroes for his role in the attack on Fort Sumter in 1861, and — of more immediate importance — he was one of the South's leading military engineers.

Beauregard arrived in Charleston on Sep-

General Pierre G. T. Beauregard considered his reassignment to Charleston a demotion. After unsuccessfully petitioning President Jefferson Davis to be restored to his command in the West, he bitterly wrote to a friend: "If the country is willing I should be put on the shelf, I will submit until our future reverses compel the Government to put me on duty."

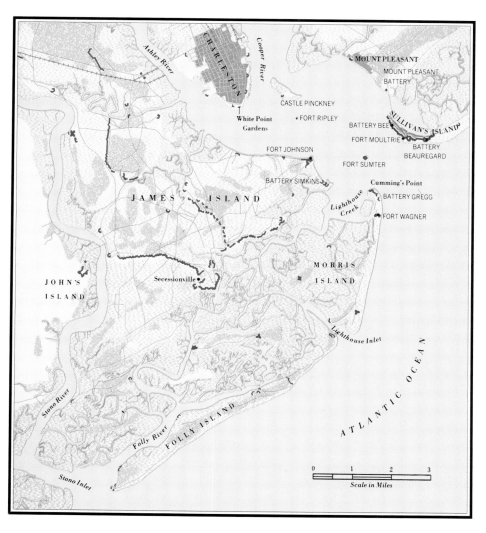

Federals advancing on Charleston faced a deadly ring of forts and batteries, anchored by Fort Sumter in midharbor. Two strategies were open to the attackers: to take James Island or Morris Island to the south by combined land and sea attack, then reduce Fort Sumter from the rear; or to send their new ironclads through the main channel to demolish the fort in a head-on assault.

Fort Wagner. And at numerous other batteries around the harbor — on James Island, at Castle Pinckney, on the waterfront in Charleston itself — Beauregard made improvements. He also placed buoys at measured distances from the forts to establish accurate firing ranges. And he salted the harbor with mines, submerged obstructions and floating webs of rope to snarl propellers. To man his defenses, he could call upon thousands of troops.

Beauregard was not content with making defensive preparations. He wanted to strike a blow at the Federal flotilla before the threatened arrival of the ironclads. On January 30, 1863, concealed batteries on the banks of the Stono River trapped the Federal gunboat *Isaac Smith* and forced her surrender. Renamed the *Stono*, the vessel joined the small Confederate defense fleet. Then, the next morning, two ironclad rams, the *Chicora* and the *Palmetto State*, steamed out of the harbor and attacked Federal ships on blockade patrol, badly damaging two of them. Beauregard seized the opportunity to declare the blockade broken. This boast was dismissed in the North, but the Confederate coup was a portent of further misfortunes for the Federal Navy at Charleston.

tember 15. Spurred by reports in the Northern press of an imminent attack on the city, he worked around the clock to add to the work done by his predecessor. At Fort Sumter, in the center of the harbor, and at Fort Moultrie, on Sullivan's Island to the north, he mounted powerful new guns. On Morris Island, at the harbor entrance, he doubled the defenses: a strongpoint called Battery Gregg sat on the island's tip; to the south, about a quarter of the way down the island, he expanded another battery into an enclosed fortification that came to be known as

The officer who was to lead the ironclad flotilla against Charleston was Rear Admiral Samuel F. Du Pont, a hale and handsome aristocrat nearing his sixtieth year. As commander of the South Atlantic Blockading Squadron and hero of the attack on the Port Royal forts, Du Pont possessed impressive credentials. As an old school Navy man who had spent his professional career commanding wooden warships, however, he was mistrustful of the newfangled machines he was to lead into Charleston Harbor. He worried about their maneuverability, their seaworthiness and their offensive capabilities against strong coastal defenses.

Each monitor mounted two guns, a 15-incher and an 11-inch Dahlgren, both in a heavily armored rotating turret. These guns were bigger than any Beauregard could bring to bear against them, but under the best of circumstances, they could be fired only once every five minutes. (As one wag put it, a man could smoke a cigar between firings.) The monitors were nearly immune to sinking by shore fire, but their delicate machinery was easily damaged. Cannonballs striking their turrets could jam the gun-rotating mechanisms and porthole shutters, leaving the vessels crippled as fighting machines.

By the end of January 1863, Du Pont had received the first monitors. To test their firepower and vulnerability, he dispatched the monitor *Montauk* against Fort McAllister, a seven-gun Confederate earthwork with an 11-inch mortar, near the mouth of the Ogeechee River on the Georgia coast. On two occasions, the *Montauk* pounded the little fort but inflicted virtually no damage. She did, however, manage to destroy the *Nashville*, a Confederate commerce raider that was grounded near the fort. Du Pont then sent down three more monitors to assault Fort McAllister. Although the ships came under heavy fire and were hit repeatedly, they suffered little injury. Yet neither did they do much harm: The fort withstood everything the ironclads could throw at it.

Rear Admiral Samuel F. Du Pont *(second from left)*, standing with his staff aboard the screw frigate *Wabash*, was faulted by Secretary of the Navy Gideon Welles for sowing pessimism about the impending attack on Charleston. Du Pont, wrote Welles, imparted "all his fears and doubts to his subordinates, until all were impressed with his apprehension."

The test only heightened Du Pont's fears. Through messages to the Navy Department, he made clear his doubts about the wisdom of a purely naval operation, suggesting instead a joint Army-Navy attack on Charleston. To Secretary Welles, Du Pont's protests seemed evidence of a lack of will — the cautions of a man who, in Welles's words, "has a reputation to preserve instead of one to make." Welles felt that the Fort McAllister attacks had been an unnecessary side show. Du Pont seemed to him to be shirking the main business of Charleston. As February and March went by with no action, Welles shared his worries with Lincoln. The President remarked that Du Pont's delays and requests for additional support reminded him of General McClellan's constant pleas for more divisions during his sluggish Peninsular Campaign.

Early in March, Welles sent Du Pont three more ironclads and a letter imploring him to get on with the attack. At last, on April 6, Du Pont ordered his fleet into action.

The flotilla consisted of seven monitors; the *Keokuk*, a lightly armored experimental ironclad mounting two 11-inch guns in twin towers; and Du Pont's flagship, the *New Ironsides*, a 3,500-ton ironclad steamer whose heavy guns were mounted in broadside. All told, the fleet boasted 32 guns, against 76 in the forts. The plan was to concentrate the fire on Fort Sumter, steaming past it to attack its northwest face. But no sooner had the fleet crossed the bar into Charleston Harbor than bad weather set in, postponing the attack until the next day.

Tidal conditions the next morning caused a further delay; it was noon before Du Pont got his slow-moving vessels into a line. The monitor *Weehawken* led the way, pushing a raft ahead of her to sweep torpedoes. To the Confederates watching from behind their batteries, the slow, stately procession must have looked more like a naval review than a prelude to battle. As the ships entered the main channel and headed for Fort Sumter, the garrison there, in a defiant gesture, raised its flags and fired a salute to the Confederacy, while the band struck up "Dixie." In Charleston itself, anxious spectators lined the docks to witness the battle in the harbor.

From the beginning, the Federal attack ran into difficulty. First the *Weehawken* tangled her anchor chain in one of the grapnels of her torpedo-sweeping raft, delaying the entire squadron for two hours. Then the *New Ironsides,* in the center of the line, had to drop anchor because she was steering erratically and her draft was so deep that she was in danger of grounding. Two of the monitors behind the flagship banged into her harmlessly, and Du Pont sent them ahead.

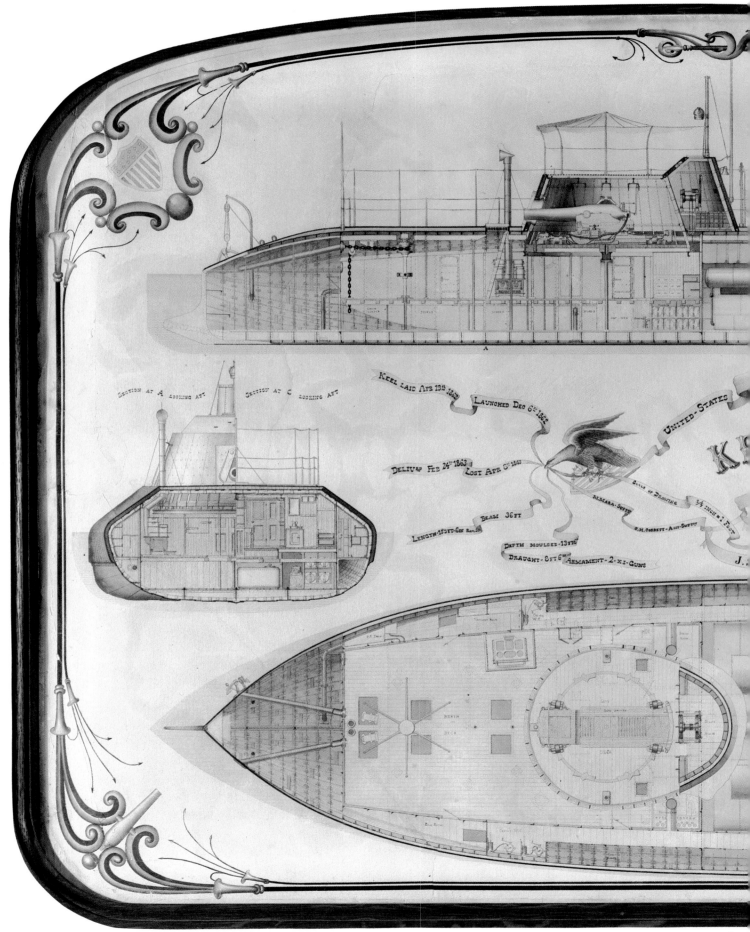

SECTION AT A LOOKING AFT   SECTION AT C LOOKING AFT

KEEL LAID APR 13TH 1862   LAUNCHED DEC 6TH 1862

DELIVD FEB 24TH 1863   LOST APR 9TH 1863

UNITED STATES

DEPTH MOULDED-13 FT
BEAM 36 FT
LENGTH-159 FT-6 IN
DRAUGHT-8 FT 6 IN   ARMAMENT-2-XI-GUNS

The Federal experimental ironclad *Keokuk,* built on this plan, was handy but vulnerable. In contrast to the low, flat, heavily armored

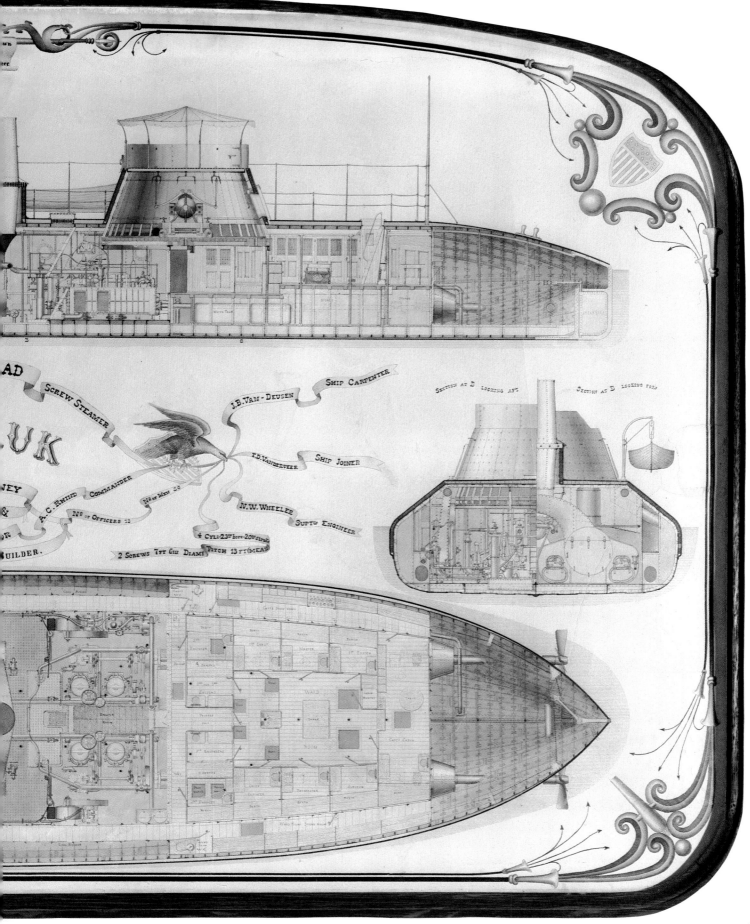

monitors, her hull was high, sloping and relatively thin-skinned. She bore two guns mounted in nonrotating, igloo-shaped towers.

He managed to get his stalled vessel under way again, only to have her immobilized in the shallow channel. Although Du Pont was unaware of it, the *New Ironsides* was now sitting directly over a huge mine — a 3,000 pound charge connected by an electric wire to Fort Wagner on Morris Island. Luckily for the ship and her crew, the detonating device did not work. The deeply frustrated Confederate engineer in charge of exploding the mine later reported that he "could not have placed the *New Ironsides* more directly over the mine if he had been allowed to, but the confounded thing, as is usual, would not go off when it was wanted."

The rest of the flotilla, meanwhile, was making little progress. The lead monitors were reluctant to pass between Forts Sumter and Moultrie for fear of entangling their propellers in the floating islands of rope that lay there. And the underwater obstructions further limited their maneuverability, holding them within the forts' field of fire. For nearly an hour, the guns on Fort Sumter blasted the ironclads, with the Confederate batteries on Sullivan's Island and Morris Island joining in to lay down a murderous cross fire. Great spouts of water shot up around the ships, and balls struck time and again on the turrets.

The Federals' return fire was sporadic at best. The *New Ironsides*, still plagued by steering problems, was too far away to be of help. Except for one parting broadside directed at Fort Moultrie, her 16 guns remained silent throughout the attack; all the while, the Confederates peppered her, scoring 55 hits, though none did serious damage.

The *Keokuk* was less fortunate. She had been the last ship in the formation at the start; in the confusion, however, she found herself leading — and closing fast on Fort Sumter. She fired three shots, but sustained much more damage than she caused. Within half an hour the *Keokuk* was transformed into a floating colander by 90 hits. With enormous difficulty, her captain maneuvered the vessel out of the action. She was to sink the next day in the shallow waters off Morris Island.

The ironclads hit Fort Sumter 55 times, cratering her ramparts, but the fort's fighting capacity remained unimpaired. All told, the ponderous ships got off only 139 shots during the entire engagement, compared with 2,200 from the defenders' batteries. More than 300 shells from Forts Sumter and Moultrie and other emplacements found their marks. Casualties were light — four dead and 10 wounded for the Confederates, one dead and 22 wounded for the Federals.

At about 5 p.m., from his station on the *New Ironsides*, Du Pont signaled a withdrawal. In spite of the day's dismal failure, the admiral planned to renew the engagement the next morning. But at a captains' conference aboard the flagship that night, he learned the full extent of the damage to his fleet: The *Weehawken* had been struck 53 times, the *Nahant* 36 times, the *Passaic* 35, the *Montauk* 14, the *Patapsco* 47, the *Catskill* 20, the *Nantucket* 51. Several of the turrets could not be rotated, and a few guns were disabled. And the *Keokuk* would soon be lying in water up to her towers. Du Pont excused himself and retired to his stateroom. During the night he made the decision not to renew the attack. "We have met with a sad repulse," he told his captains. "I shall not turn it into a great disaster." Without exception, the officers supported him. "The ironclad captains," his chief of staff later wrote, "stood like a wall of iron about Admiral Du Pont's reputation, and there was no joint to be pierced in their armor.''

In Charleston and throughout the South, the rout of the ironclads brought great rejoicing. In Washington, there were only recriminations. Lincoln, Welles and Fox all blamed Du Pont for the failure. ''After all our outlay and great preparations,'' Welles scornfully wrote, ''giving him all our force, and a large portion of our best officers, a fight of 30 minutes and the loss of one man satisfied the admiral.''

Du Pont was to suffer one more humiliation. Outside Charleston Harbor, about 1,300 yards off Morris Island, lay the wreck of the *Keokuk*, her smokestacks visible even at high tide. If the Confederates could salvage her two 11-inch guns, they might be used to defend the city. General Beauregard decided to try to retrieve them. A crew of riggers directed by Adolphus W. La Coste, a civilian engineer, began the perilous operation, working only at night and at low tide.

Just off the bar stood the Federal blockading fleet; a dropped hammer or crowbar might be enough to bring the riggers under the fire of the gunboats. But night after night, through late April and early May, the

Belching smoke from their guns, vessels of the Federal ironclad fleet attack Fort Sumter on April 7, 1863. The unarmed craft in the foreground is the U.S. Coast Survey steamship *Bibb,* which carried newspaper reporters.

men labored on, clinging to the slippery towers while they struggled to cut away metal and free the guns. Their mission did not remain a secret: One night the Federals opened a barrage upon them, and the Confederate ram *Chicora*, guarding the salvage team, returned the fire. For unknown reasons, the Federals failed to press the attack. Finally, after two weeks of intensive labor, the two 13-foot-long, eight-ton guns were raised with block and tackle and successfully transferred to Charleston's defenses. One of the 11-inchers was mounted at Fort Sumter and the other on Sullivan's Island.

The salvage of the *Keokuk's* guns was the *coup de grâce* for Du Pont. Secretary Welles sent him an angry letter, blaming him for neglecting "the duty of destroying the *Keokuk* and preventing her guns from falling into the hands of the rebels." Soon after, Du Pont resigned his command. Rear Admiral Andrew H. Foote, who had earned a reputation as an aggressive fighter while commanding the Western Flotilla, was selected to replace Du Pont. But Foote was seriously ill at the time, and he died before he could assume his new post. The assignment then fell to Rear Admiral John A. Dahlgren, the 54-year-old ordnance expert and inventor of the bottle-shaped gun that bore his name.

The failure of the ironclads meant that U.S. Army troops, who had landed on Folly Island, would have to join the Navy in attacking Charleston and its forts. No longer would the soldiers be viewed as mere occupiers. They would have to fight.

The man who would lead Federal land forces in the assault on Charleston was Major General Quincy Adams Gillmore. He replaced

Rear Admiral John A. Dahlgren, leaning against the naval gun he designed, had not been assigned to sea duty for nearly two decades when he succeeded Du Pont at Charleston in July 1863. His appointment irked old Navy men — especially Du Pont, who privately scorned him as a desk sailor who "ate cream" while those in action were "eating dirt."

General David Hunter as commander of the Department of the South in June 1863. Gillmore, an engineer, was experienced in siege operations. He had sited the batteries that had subdued Fort Pulaski, downriver from Savannah, after only two days of bombardment, proving that the mightiest fortress was no match for rifled guns fired from fixed land positions. He was now ready to teach Fort Sumter the same lesson.

The strategy, worked out in Washington, called for Gillmore's forces on Folly Island to cross narrow Lighthouse Inlet and land on the beach at the south end of Morris Island. Then the troops would advance up the four-mile length of the island, overwhelm Fort

Wagner and Battery Gregg at its northern end, and there establish artillery emplacements from which Fort Sumter could be reduced to rubble. Deprived of its key fortress, Charleston could then be taken by Dahlgren's fleet. In pursuing this plan, which was to prove deeply flawed, the Federals would open one of the War's bloodiest chapters.

Shortly after daybreak on July 10, Gillmore's batteries on Folly Island began a two-hour bombardment of the Confederate defenses on the southern end of Morris Island. Then Gillmore sent a brigade across Lighthouse Inlet under the covering fire of four monitors offshore. In the first launch was

Brigadier General George C. Strong, a handsome young West Pointer who had graduated with high honors and was now keen to prove himself as a battlefield commander.

As Confederate shells churned up the surf around them, the men hit the beach, some of them wading ashore. Strong was so eager to get at the foe that he leaped into water over his head and had to be fished out by his men, minus boots and hat. Strong's brigade surged forward, taking the first line of defenses, then the second. The Confederates were forced to withdraw up the narrow beach toward Fort Wagner.

By 9 a.m., the Federals had pushed to

Flanked by his staff, General Quincy Adams Gillmore, commander of land forces for the assault on Charleston, studies a map on Morris Island. When Gillmore criticized the Navy's tactics, Secretary Welles described him as having "the infirmities which belong to those trained to secondary positions. They blame others without the faculty of accomplishing great results themselves."

Federal tents rise from the dunes of Folly Island, where a supply depot has been established. In the background, ships from Northern ports wait to be unloade•

within several hundred yards of the fort, only to be stopped by heavy fire. The fort was defended by 1,300 men — the 51st and 31st North Carolina Regiments, the Charleston Battalion and several companies of South Carolina artillerymen — under the command of Brigadier General William B. Taliaferro. Yet despite their show of resistance, the undermanned garrison was in disarray, demoralized by the rapidity of the Federal advance. If Gillmore's troops had stormed the fort that day, they might have taken it. But his men were exhausted, and Gillmore chose to delay the assault until the next morning.

To the naked eye, Fort Wagner was little more than a series of irregular, low sand hills. But it was a more formidable installation than it appeared. Beneath the heaped-up sand was a core of timber and sandbags. This structure could absorb artillery projectiles without any real damage; whatever sand was displaced could be shoveled back again. The fort mounted eleven heavy guns in fixed positions and a number of mobile fieldpieces that could be quickly run into place wherever they were needed. Behind the parapets, Beauregard had built a huge bombproof, where some 750 men could retire during heavy artillery bombardments. He had also extended the fort, so that it stretched 800 feet from the ocean on the east to a marsh on the west. Battery Gregg protected its rear. The only possible approach was up the beach from the south, and spring storms had narrowed the width of the beach in front of the fort to about 100 feet.

Gillmore planned to renew the attack with Strong's brigade again in the vanguard; the 7th Connecticut would lead, followed by the 76th Pennsylvania and the 9th Maine. Before dawn, the men of the 7th formed up. Strong instructed them not to pause to reload as they charged, but to storm the fortress with fixed bayonets — a chilling order to these soldiers, who were not yet battle-hardened. "When I learned what we were to do, my knees shook so that I thought I should drop," a private later wrote.

At daybreak, the men advanced in silence, but when the Confederates opened fire, the attackers raised a yell and charged, jumping into the moat that fronted the fort, sloshing through the sea water, and scrambling up the other side to make straight for the parapet. There they were stopped.

Pinned down by small-arms fire, the 7th huddled under the parapet, waiting for support that never came. The 76th and 9th, raked by musket fire, hesitated to make their charge. The isolated men of the 7th were doomed whether they advanced or retreated, and most chose to retreat. Those few who had made it to the top of the parapet were perfect targets against the early-morning sky. All told, the Federals lost 339 men, with the gallant 7th losing about half of its complement. The Confederates suffered only 12 casualties.

The action might have convinced Gillmore that Fort Wagner was impervious to direct infantry assault, but he decided to try once more before settling down to siege operations. This time, however, he would first soften the position by intensive artillery bombardment. Both heavy and light guns were brought up, and Dahlgren's warships moved into position. On the 18th of July, 41 of Gillmore's guns, together with the *New Ironsides*, five other monitors and five gunboats, threw an awesome barrage of shot at Fort Wagner — enough, in the words of a Connecticut sergeant, to establish "several

Brigadier General William B. Taliaferro was on duty at Savannah, Georgia, when the Federals invaded Morris Island. He took a leave of absence and rushed to Charleston to volunteer, assuming command of Fort Wagner just five days before the second Federal assault.

Brigadier General George C. Strong had been with his brigade for only a few weeks when he was mortally wounded leading a charge against Fort Wagner, but his example left a lasting impression on his troops. A soldier wrote: "He never asked men to go where he did not lead the way."

Black troops of the 54th Massachusetts battle hand to hand with Confederate defenders on the parapet of Fort Wagner on July 18, 1863. Proclaimed one of the 54th's white officers: "The genius of Dante could but faintly portray the horrors of that hell."

first class iron foundries." Eventually the defenders stopped replying. The bombardment ended, and the Federals prepared for an evening attack.

Gillmore assigned overall responsibility to Brigadier General Truman Seymour, an officer of the garrison that had surrendered Fort Sumter at the start of the War. Seymour was grimly determined to see that fort restored to the Union. He tapped General Strong, who had shown great courage in the previous assault, to lead seven regiments in the first wave of the attack. A second wave would be composed of four regiments commanded by one of Strong's West Point classmates, Colonel Haldimand S. Putnam. And a third wave of four regiments was to be led by Brigadier General Thomas G. Stevenson.

Strong chose a newly arrived regiment to spearhead the charge — the 54th Massachusetts, a black regiment commanded by Colonel Robert Gould Shaw, a slight, blond, 25-year-old Boston Brahmin whose abolitionist mother, as she watched the 54th march proudly out of Boston late in May, had cried out, "What have I done that God has been so good to me!"

The regiment, led by young whites and manned by freedmen (including two sons of Frederick Douglass), had seen little fighting and was distrusted by many military men, who doubted the ability of blacks to fight. So when General Strong offered to let the 54th lead, Shaw eagerly accepted. Here was the opportunity to prove the caliber of his men.

Shaw's adjutant, Lieutenant Garth W.

Colonel Robert Gould Shaw, son of a wealthy Boston abolitionist, leads the black 54th Massachusetts off to war in this heroic bas-relief by Augustus Saint-Gaudens. On watching the departure of the regiment from Boston, the poet John Greenleaf Whittier paid tribute to its young commander: "The very flower of grace and chivalry, he seemed to me beautiful and awful, as an angel of God come down to lead the host of freedom to victory."

James, the younger brother of the illustrious Henry and William James, described the moments before the charge: "General Strong, mounted on a superb gray charger, in full dress, white gloves, a yellow bandana handkerchief coiled around his neck, approached Colonel Shaw to give the final orders." Strong addressed the 54th and pointed at one of the color-bearers. "If this man should fall, who will lift the flag and carry it on?" he demanded. "I will," replied Colonel Shaw, taking a cigar from between his teeth. The men cheered. When Strong rode off to bring up the rest of the brigade, Shaw told the regiment, "I want you to prove yourselves. The eyes of thousands will look on what you do tonight." Then he drew his sword and led them forward.

Almost immediately it became obvious that the bombardment of the sand fortress had failed to subdue the Confederate garrison. Emerging from their bombproof, the Confederates loosed a torrent of shot and shell on the black troops, who were forced to advance in column of companies rather than line of battle on the narrow beach. The soldiers were so tightly wedged together, elbow to elbow, that the bullets and shells from the fort could hardly fail to hit a target. Men fell on all sides as the quick step became a double-quick and then a full run.

Shaw, in the lead, splashed through the moat and gained the walls of the fort. With him was a chunky, 23-year-old black private, William H. Carney, who reported that "the shot — grape, canister and hand grenades — came in showers, and the columns were leveled." Shaw was shot through the heart atop the parapet and toppled headlong into the fort. The color-bearers went down as well,

Still recovering from his wounds, Sergeant William H. Carney of the 54th Massachusetts displays the flag that he saved from capture when the assault on Fort Wagner failed. For his bravery under fire, Carney was awarded the Congressional Medal of Honor shown below.

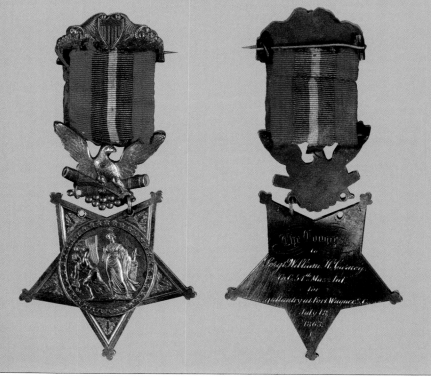

and the state flag was torn from its staff by a jubilant Confederate. Carney, though wounded twice and covered with blood, picked up the U.S. flag and managed to drag it from the field. For this act he would be awarded the Congressional Medal of Honor — the first black to be so honored.

As the 54th fell back in disorder, the rest of Strong's brigade came up. Some of the soldiers of the 6th Connecticut and the 48th New York managed to climb to the top of the bombproof and the eastern redoubt of the fort, where they engaged the Confederates hand to hand.

Down the beach General Strong, sword in hand, decided to bring up the 76th Pennsylvania. As he raised the cry, "Forward Seventy-Sixth!" he went down with a ragged shrapnel wound in his thigh; two weeks later he would die of that wound.

Now the second wave — Colonel Putnam's regiments — entered the fray. Reaching the fort, they found a jumble of Federal dead and wounded, black and white alike. Putnam clambered onto the redoubt, beyond which — atop the bombproof — remnants of Strong's regiments were holding their own against the Confederate defenders. In the gathering gloom, one of Putnam's regiments mistook the Federals on the fortress for the enemy and shot into their midst. Hit by the defenders in front and the attackers coming up behind them, Federals fell by the dozens. As darkness came, the survivors huddled on the piled-up bodies of their fallen comrades. Putnam had been shot dead along with most of his officers, and at dawn, finding themselves surrounded by the fort's defenders, the surviving Federals surrendered.

During the bloody attack, messages had been sent to the rear urging that the third wave, under Thomas Stevenson, be brought up. But Seymour had been wounded, and General Gillmore was so shaken by his losses that he refused to commit any more troops.

It had been a massacre. The Federals had lost 1,515 killed, wounded or missing. Confederate casualties amounted to 174 men. In the morning, the men of Fort Wagner buried hundreds of Federals in mass graves. When a party under a flag of truce asked the fort's new commander, Brigadier General Johnson Hagood, to return Colonel Shaw's body, he reportedly answered, "We have buried him in the trench with his niggers." Later Shaw's father wrote General Gillmore, asking him to make no special attempt to recover his son.

The father declared, "We can imagine no holier place than that in which he is, among his brave and devoted followers, nor wish for him better company."

In ten days on Morris Island, General Gillmore had lost one third of his men, and the capture of Fort Wagner, his immediate goal, seemed as remote as ever. Instead of risking another frontal attack, Gillmore decided to try what he trusted would be a less costly method of forcing the garrison's surrender. He would lay siege to it. Sappers would dig zigzag trenches in front of the parapet, and slowly Gillmore's big guns would be brought closer and closer to the wall.

Shielded from small-arms fire by a wicker cylinder called a rolling sap, Federal sappers work their way along the beach toward Fort Wagner.

A detail from the 39th Illinois prepares to load their Requa battery gun, a novel weapon consisting of 25 barrels mounted on a field carriage. The Requas were in the trenches near Fort Wagner to protect sappers from Confederate sharpshooters.

At Gillmore's command was an impressive array of artillery pieces of the most modern design, including a new weapon, the Requa battery gun—a so-called volley gun, made up of 25 rifle barrels so arranged on a frame that they could discharge 175 shots per minute. Another novelty was the calcium floodlight, whose brilliant white beam was produced by playing a very hot flame on lime. Gillmore used this device to illuminate the ramparts of Fort Wagner. The floodlight enabled the Federals to continue the bombardment at night, while virtually blinding the enemy so that fire could not be accurately returned. It also allowed the Federals to keep watch against nighttime attacks on their entrenchments, and to take aim on enemy soldiers trying to make repairs on Wagner's parapet under cover of darkness.

The digging of zigzag trenches and the emplacement of the big guns were hercu-lean tasks. The shallow sand covering the island lay on a base of mud, which made it very difficult to stabilize the heavy artillery. To make matters worse, Confederate sharpshooters using high-powered rifles with telescopic sights proved expert at picking off the sappers. It was worth a man's life to stick his head above the lip of the trench. In retaliation, Gillmore created his own detachment of sharpshooters.

As the trench work progressed, the sappers began accidentally to dig out the buried remains of their comrades killed in the two infantry assaults. At first they attempted to reinter the corpses, but soon they gave that up and instead moved them to one side and covered them so that they became part of the trench walls, a grisly task that added one more element of misery to the daily routine.

By early September, Gillmore was bombarding the fort from artillery positions near-

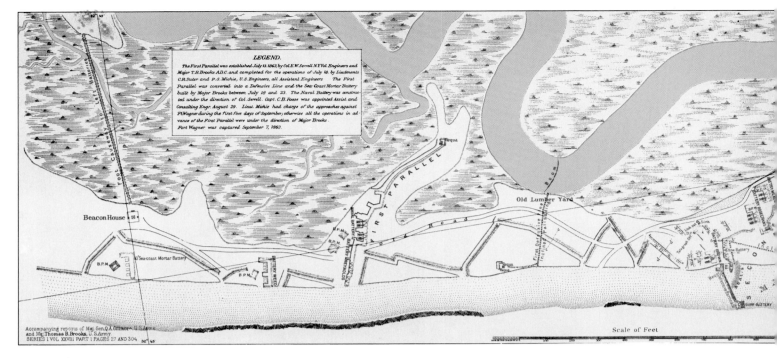

LEGEND.

The First Parallel was established July 13, 1863, by Col. E.W. Serrell N.Y. Vol. Engineers and Major T.B. Brooks A.D.C. and completed for the operations of July 18. by Lieutenants C.R. Suter and P.S. Michie, U.S. Engineers, all Assistant Engineers. The First Parallel was converted into a Defensive Line and the Sea-Coast Mortar Battery built by Major Brooks between July 18 and 23. The Naval Battery was constructed under the direction of Col. Serrell. Capt. C.B. Reese was appointed Assist. and Consulting Engr. August 29. Lieut. Michie had charge of the approaches against Ft. Wagner during the first five days of September; otherwise all the operations in advance of the First Parallel were under the direction of Major Brooks. Fort Wagner was captured September 7, 1863.

ly as sturdy as Fort Wagner itself. And his forward guns were mounted within point-blank range of the Confederate bastion.

Inside the fort, conditions were growing intolerable. The bombproof, where temperatures rose to well above 100 degrees, was a place of last resort. A field hospital was established there for the wounded, and as the battle grew more intense, the screams of the dying in the bombproof were punctuated by the booming reports of artillery fire. The fort's wells were polluted by the decomposing corpses buried nearby, making the meager supply of fresh water that was shipped in from Charleston the most precious of commodities.

The Federal barrage was augmented by Dahlgren's ironclads, still stationed off the fort's sea wall. Navy gunners grew expert at placing their shells precisely on target. They even learned how to skip shells off the surface of the water to bring them into the deepest recesses of the fort.

As Gillmore brought his guns closer to the strongpoint, he also drew within range of mighty Fort Sumter. Gillmore decided to concentrate his long-range rifles on that target. The bombardment of Fort Sumter, one of the most intense yet known to warfare,

began at dawn on August 17, 1863, and continued unabated for seven days. During the first 24 hours, the Federals hurled 948 shells at the fort, 678 of which found their mark. Day after day, the pounding went on with scarcely a letup. Dahlgren moved his ironclads as close as he dared in order to support Gillmore's fire.

Fort Sumter's gunners fought back as best they could. On the first day of the bombardment, a Confederate shell hit the pilothouse of the monitor *Catskill*, its impact knocking loose a piece of iron that went rocketing through the cabin. The fragment struck both Captain George W. Rodgers — Dahlgren's chief of staff — and the ship's assistant paymaster, killing them both. But that was a random hit. General Beauregard in Charleston soon realized that Fort Sumter was no match for the combined firepower of the monitors and Gillmore's land-based, long-range rifles. He judged that the masonry walls of the fort could not long hold out against such a blizzard of iron, and removed as many of its guns as he could by boat. By August 23, Fort Sumter had ceased replying to the Federal guns. "Not a single gun remained in barbette," Beauregard reported to the Confederate War Department, "and but

This official U.S. Army map shows the positions of the elaborate Federal works established on Morris Island by General Gillmore during the assault on Fort Wagner *(right)*. Following classic siege warfare techniques, Gillmore dug trenches in a zigzag pattern, rather than straight ahead, to prevent the fort's defenders from enfilading his lines — firing directly down them.

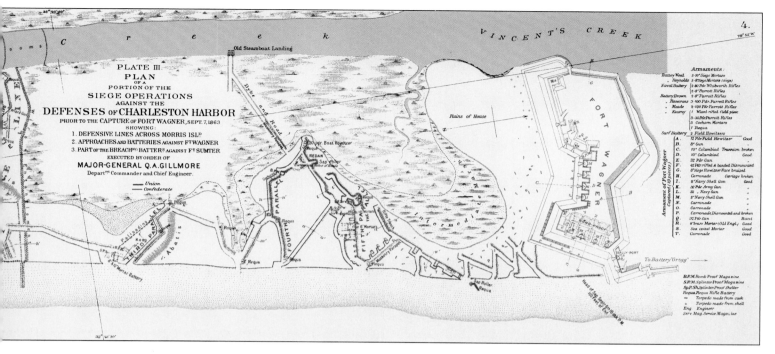

PLATE III.
PLAN
OF A
PORTION OF THE
SIEGE OPERATIONS
AGAINST THE
DEFENSES OF CHARLESTON HARBOR
PRIOR TO THE CAPTURE OF FORT WAGNER, SEPT. 7, 1863
SHOWING:
1. DEFENSIVE LINES ACROSS MORRIS ISL^D
2. APPROACHES AND BATTERIES AGAINST F^T WAGNER
3. PART OF THE BREACH^ING BATTER^S AGAINST F^T SUMTER
EXECUTED BY ORDER OF
MAJOR-GENERAL Q.A.GILLMORE
Depart^mt Commander and Chief Engineer.

a single smooth-bore 32-pounder in the west face could be fired."

Gillmore triumphantly reported to Washington on August 24: "Fort Sumter is today a shapeless and harmless mass of ruins." It only remained now to take Fort Wagner. By early September, the Federal line was within shouting distance of the stronghold. On September 5, backed by the ironclads, Gillmore's batteries opened an intensive two-day bombardment. The endurance of the defenders was close to the breaking point, and on the 6th, Colonel Lawrence M. Keitt, now the commander of Fort Wagner, sent a message to Beauregard reporting that he had only 400 soldiers left who could fight.

Now that Gillmore's guns had blasted Fort Sumter into rubble, Fort Wagner and Battery Gregg were hardly worth the sacrifice of 400 lives. Beauregard ordered an evacuation, getting men and guns out by boat on the night of September 6. The next morning, Gillmore's troops stormed the fort and found it deserted. The heroic resistance had come to an end. A small Confederate force had held off a Federal army 10 times its size for almost two months. In the process, the attackers had suffered 2,300 casualties.

Admiral Dahlgren now laid plans to cap-

ture the ruined Fort Sumter. Occupying it once and for all would prevent the Confederates from remounting guns there. And running up the Stars and Stripes at this bastion of Southern resistance would provide a tremendous morale boost for the North — soldier and civilian alike. Gillmore was planning a separate assault using Army troops. Coordination between the services had, for the time being, collapsed.

The Navy's operation got under way first. Dahlgren had been cheered by reports indicating that Fort Sumter's garrison was insignificant and that only token resistance could be expected. Such was his confidence that when Commander Thomas Stevens, chosen to lead the assault, protested that it was too risky, the admiral replied: "You have only to go in and take possession. You will find nothing but a corporal's guard."

The Confederate artillerymen at Fort Sumter had been withdrawn and replaced by about 320 infantrymen, under Major Stephen Elliott Jr. To Beauregard, the bastion was still vital to Charleston's defenses. In his orders to Elliott, he wrote: "You are to be sent to a fort deprived of all offensive capacity, and having but one gun — a 32-pounder — with which to salute the flag. But

Firing on Fort Sumter from a distance of more than two miles, a Federal gunner prepares to pull the lanyard of a 100-pounder Parrott rifle (*left*) at Battery Stevens on Morris Island. Nearby, crew members seated beside a dismounted gun tube set the fuses on shells.

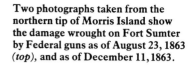

Two photographs taken from the northern tip of Morris Island show the damage wrought on Fort Sumter by Federal guns as of August 23, 1863 (*top*), and as of December 11, 1863.

that fort is Fort Sumter, the key to the entrance of this harbor. It must be held to the bitter end, not with artillery, but with infantry alone; and there can be no hope of reinforcements."

As a prelude to the landing, Dahlgren called for the fort's immediate surrender, an ultimatum peremptorily refused by Beauregard. He replied: "Inform Admiral Dahlgren that he may have Fort Sumter when he can take it and hold it."

On the night of September 8, a volunteer force of 500 sailors and Marines embarked from Federal warships in small boats for Fort Sumter. The party was still well offshore when Confederate sentinels at the ruins spotted the boats and spread the alarm. Shore batteries on James Island and Sullivan's Island opened up on the invaders, as did the Confederate ram *Chicora,* while infantry hidden in the rubble maintained a steady musket fire on the approaching boats.

"The air was blazing with bursting shells," recalled Commander Stevens, "and the ear was deafened with the roar of cannon, the rattle of musketry, the whistling of grape, and the explosion of hand grenades." Those men who managed to land were swiftly cut down or captured.

Stevens ordered a withdrawal, but five of his boats were seized. All told, the Navy lost 124 men to this "corporal's guard." Gillmore, whose own assault on Fort Sumter had been delayed, hastily canceled the entire operation when he learned of the Navy's fiasco.

For Dahlgren, a quandary remained. He could try to push his ironclads past Fort Sumter and the still-dangerous Confederate batteries on Sullivan's and James Islands to put the city under his guns. But to do so involved risks that the admiral was quite unwilling to take. Suppose a shot from an island battery were to disable one of his ironclads, leading to its capture? Once repaired by the

Confederates, the ship would certainly be employed in their behalf to play havoc with the wooden vessels on blockade duty. Although the admiral offered to go in and try again if Secretary Welles would send him three more monitors, the government decided the hazards were no longer worth the prize. In the aftermath of Federal victories elsewhere, at Vicksburg and Gettysburg, Washington realized that Charleston's capture was no longer of the first importance.

Dahlgren must have been relieved. After weeks of fighting, he was physically and mentally exhausted. Confinement aboard an iron ship in the sweltering Carolina heat had taken its toll. Seasickness, frustration and a sense of failure gnawed at him. "The worst of this place is that one only stops getting weaker. One does not get stronger," he noted in his journal. "My debility increases, so that today it is an exertion to sit in a chair. I do not see well. How strange — no pain, but so feeble. It seems like gliding away to death. How easy it seems! Why not, to one whose race is run?"

With the Navy unwilling to risk its ironclads and the Army equally hesitant to move on the city without massive reinforcements, the situation lapsed into a stalemate. Yet there was no relief from the horror. The Union was too committed to its campaign against Charleston to withdraw entirely. To have done so would have been a terrible blow to Federal pride.

Fort Sumter remained the focus of Federal fury. To prevent the Confederates from mounting new guns, the pitiful pile of debris was subjected to months of bombardments from both the ironclads and the Federal batteries now established on the sites of Battery Gregg and Fort Wagner. For 41 days and nights, beginning on October 26, 1863, Federal guns blasted the fort, doing little more than shifting the rubble from one site to another. On just one day, a single gun on Morris Island poured seven and a half tons of metal into the fort. But as it turned out, the heaviest casualties at the Confederate strongpoint were inflicted not by the Federals but by the defenders themselves.

Early that December, Fort Sumter's beleaguered garrison received an unaccustomed respite from bombardment. The men busied themselves improving their defenses, and when time and weather permitted, they relaxed under the thin rays of the late autumn sun. As most of the walls of the fort were no longer standing, the garrison had used the debris to construct an intricate series of protective tunnels between the living quarters and storage rooms. Three of these rooms were powder magazines, and at about 9:30 a.m. on December 11, the small-arms magazine exploded, sending sheets of flame through the rubble-lined corridors, killing 11 men and wounding 41.

No one knows what started the inferno. There were rumors that a candle ignited some whiskey fumes, which in turn set off the ammunition; or it may have been a spark from a soldier's pipe. Whatever the cause, the fire raged out of control in the caverns. The men tried to wall off the affected corridors, but the heat was so intense that their barricades virtually disintegrated. They could only allow the fire to burn itself out, and hope that the enemy would not seize this chance to launch another attack.

As it happened, the Federals did not react immediately. Because the fire was burning within the tunnels, lookouts on Morris Island saw only thin wisps of smoke rising from Fort Sumter that morning. Eventually word did reach the Federal forces that something disastrous had occurred, and then the guns on Morris Island opened up. In a few hours more than 200 shells fell on the garrison. By midafternoon, however, the fire had been confined. The garrison's commander, hoping to rebuild the morale of his stricken force, summoned the band to the parapet, and the musicians struck up "Dixie." As the music drifted across the water to Morris Island, the Federal gunners, in a rare display of sympathy between the opposing forces, suspended their bombardment and raised a cheer for Fort Sumter's brave defenders.

Meanwhile, the citizens of Charleston were feeling the heat of Federal wrath. In late August, before the surrender of the Mor-

ris Island batteries, General Gillmore had launched a campaign of terror against the city. The general had ordered an eight-inch, 200-pounder Parrott rifle to be emplaced in a Morris Island marsh, armed with shells carrying a brand of the incendiary substance known as Greek fire, and trained on Charleston, with a church steeple as the point of aim. Mounting this Swamp Angel, as the Parrott rifle was dubbed by its crew, proved to be a major engineering feat. Over a trestle road that was laid two and a half miles through the swamp, 2,300 men carried 13,000 sandbags, a total of 800 tons of sand. At the terminus of this causeway, pilings were sunk 20 feet into the mud until they reached firm ground, and on these a platform was constructed. Around it the sandbags were heaped high to form a battery, and the 16,500-pound Parrott rifle was

Charleston photographer George S. Cook took this picture from inside Fort Sumter on September 8, 1863, just as a shell fired by a Federal ironclad exploded on the rubble-strewn parade ground. At left, some of the defenders can be seen sitting and standing amid the ruins.

Terrified civilians in Charleston duck for cover as the first shell fired from the Federal Parrott rifle known as the Swamp Angel explodes above a street at 1:30 a.m. on August 22, 1863. Other than setting one house ablaze, the 16 shots fired at the city that night caused little damage.

hauled over the marsh and emplaced inside.

The soldiers who performed this labor, besides contending with heat and mosquitoes, were harassed by fire from three Confederate batteries on James Island. Some of the Federals were used as decoys, working on a dummy battery some distance from the real one to draw the enemy's fire. Throughout all this labor and danger, the men managed to keep their sense of humor. When the Swamp Angel was finally ready, a story went the rounds that Gillmore was now looking for "20 men, 18 feet long, to do duty in 15 feet of mud."

By August 21, during the great bombardment of Fort Sumter, Gillmore was ready to shell the city. He dispatched a message to Beauregard demanding the immediate surrender of Morris Island and Fort Sumter. "Should you refuse compliance, or should I receive no reply within four hours,"

he wrote, "I shall open fire on the city of Charleston."

Beauregard was away inspecting Charleston's fortifications when the demand arrived at his headquarters, and since no answer came within the allotted time, Gillmore carried out his threat at 1:30 a.m. on August 22. The Swamp Angel's gun crew knew their first shot was on target when bells in the city began to jangle and whistles screeched. Beauregard sent an angry dispatch to Gillmore, accusing him of turning his guns "against the old men, the women and children, and the hospitals of a sleeping city— an act of inexcusable barbarity." After the War, Gillmore offered a succinct justification for his action: "Charleston had been besieged for seven weeks, was occupied by the enemy's troops and batteries; gunboats had been built and were then building along its waterfront, and the avenue of escape for noncombatants was open and undisputed."

The Parrott rifle immediately achieved its purpose of spreading terror. In the streets of the waterfront, people streamed out of their homes and raced for the upper city to get out of range. Next morning, the British consul in Charleston appeared at Gillmore's headquarters to lodge a protest against the shelling. Gillmore refused to receive him, and the bombardment continued. Soon, however, it became apparent to the citizens that most of Gillmore's incendiary shells were not very effective, and disdain for the Federal gunners replaced panic. Banks and hospitals moved out of the impact zone, but most resi-

dents refused to be budged, keeping tubs of water in their homes to fight fires.

In the North, the news that the city was under bombardment prompted general rejoicing. The fact that the War had reached a new and ominous stage with the deliberate shelling of a civilian population caused little soul-searching. A Federal officer summed up Northern sentiment when he wrote: "What a wonderful retaliation! Frightened inhabitants fleeing from the wrath of a just avenger." And New York diarist George Templeton Strong could barely contain his glee. "She deserves it all," he wrote of Charleston. "Sowing the wind was an exhila-

Federal soldiers guard the remains of the Swamp Angel at its battery in a marsh on Morris Island, about four miles from Charleston. The piece exploded while firing its 36th shot against the city. The force of the explosion blew the gun tube forward onto the parapet.

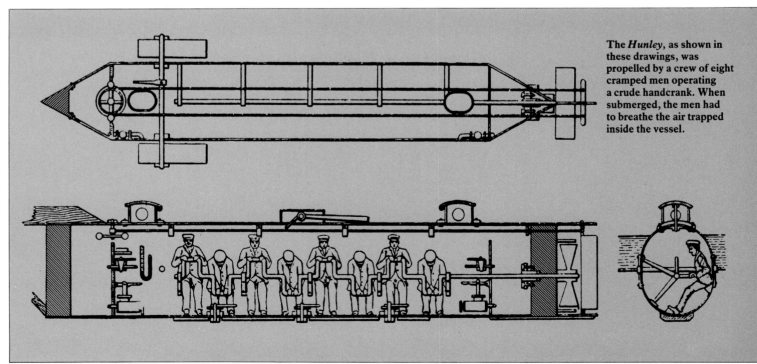

The *Hunley*, as shown in these drawings, was propelled by a crew of eight cramped men operating a crude handcrank. When submerged, the men had to breathe the air trapped inside the vessel.

rating chivalric pastime. Resisting the whirlwind is less agreeable."

For all that, the Swamp Angel had a brief career. To reach its distant target, the piece had to be charged with 20 pounds of powder, four more than the normal charge. Perhaps because of this, several shells exploded prematurely in the tube, weakening the gun. As it fired its 36th round, the Swamp Angel blew up.

After the Federals gained control of Morris Island, Gillmore set up new batteries at Cumming's Point on the northern tip and resumed the bombardment, laying waste to much of the lower city. During nine days in January 1864, some 1,500 shells would be hurled at Charleston. Yet each shell seemed only to increase the determination of soldiers and civilians to resist and strike back.

Frustrated in his attempts to take Charleston, Gillmore in December 1863 suggested that his Department of the South be assigned another, more promising coastal expedition. The general proposed to ship a portion of the troops at Charleston to northern Florida, where they would impose a pro-Federal government. Confederate opposition was expected to be light, and the Lincoln administration gave the go-ahead.

On February 7, 1864, Brigadier General Truman Seymour's 7,000-man division landed at Jacksonville on the Florida coast and began marching west into the interior to engage the Confederates. On February 20, Seymour led 5,500 of his men in a poorly planned assault on a force of about 4,600 Confederates near the hamlet of Olustee. His attacks were piecemeal; the Confederates stood firm and then counterattacked. Led by Irish-born Brigadier General Joseph Fine-

gan, they swept forward in a charge that drove Seymour's disorganized army from the field. The 8th United States Colored Troops, one of three black regiments in Seymour's force, lost 310 men, including 87 killed or mortally wounded. The campaign had been an unmitigated failure.

The Federal force at Charleston, meanwhile, was having problems of its own. For the Confederates there had begun retaliating with some novel weapons. On the night of October 5, 1863, a peculiar craft had steamed out of the harbor. Christened the *David*, this cigar-shaped, 50-foot-long vessel, bearing a torpedo on a spar at its bow, was on a mission of extreme danger and great import — to sink the *New Ironsides*. Riding so low in the water that she was nearly invisible, the *David* got to within 50 yards of her quarry before a sharp-eyed lookout spotted her. Challenged, a crewman on the *David* replied with a blast from a shotgun, and the attacking vessel proceeded toward the great ship at full speed.

As Federals peppered the waters around her with small-arms fire, the *David* rammed her torpedo against the *New Ironsides'* hull. Then came the explosion of 60 pounds of powder, not enough to disable the Federal vessel but more than enough to send her into port for repairs. The incident alarmed U.S. Navy officers, who feared that next time the torpedo might carry a heavier charge. The *David*, which made good its escape, became the model for several sister ships, but the War ended before they could see action.

On February 17, 1864, an even stranger craft threatened the Federal blockaders. This was the hand-cranked, experimental submarine *H. L. Hunley*, built from a 25-foot-long boiler cylinder. During trial runs,

139

This damaged Confederate torpedo boat was one of eight such craft financed privately in Charleston. Built for a crew of four on the plan of the *David*, the steam-powered boats were 50 feet long, with a bow spar carrying a 60-pound charge. They could be partly submerged.

the *Hunley* had sunk several times, taking the lives of at least 32 crewmen; the vessel had been called "the peripatetic coffin." On the night of the 17th, bearing a torpedo on a bow spar, the *Hunley*—barely visible in the full moonlight—pushed toward the wooden sloop-of-war *Housatonic*, on blockade duty outside the harbor.

At about 9 p.m., the *Housatonic's* acting master suddenly noticed a rippling on the water and then spotted the submarine herself. He gave the alarm, but the *Hunley* was so close that the *Housatonic's* guns could not be brought to bear. The little vessel pressed on through rifle fire to ram the gunboat with her torpedo. There was a tremendous explosion; the entire stern of the *Housatonic* disintegrated, and as the crew scrambled into boats, the ship went to the bottom. The *Hunley*, true to her nickname, also went down, taking her crewmen to their graves.

Though the *David* and the *Hunley* opened a new chapter in the history of naval warfare, they were hardly sufficient in themselves to alter the situation at Charleston. Yet neither were the attacking Federals able to devise a combination of tactics that would swing the balance in their favor. For all the sacrifices, for all the carnage, it is unlikely that the campaign along the rim of Charleston's outer harbor shortened the War by so much as a day.

When, at last, on the night of February 17, 1865, the Confederate troops finally evacuated their positions, and the city of Charleston fell, it was neither the Federal ironclads nor the troops on Morris Island that forced the issue, but the approach of General William Tecumseh Sherman's army, marching northward from Georgia.

Battles on Two Coasts

"It is a curious sight to catch a single shot from a piece of ordnance. You see the shot coming. The inclination to do reverence is so strong that it is almost impossible to resist."

ACTING ASSISTANT SURGEON WILLIAM F. HUTCHINSON, U.S.S. *LACKAWANNA*, AT MOBILE BAY

By the summer of 1864, the Federals had taken all but two of their principal objectives in the coastal war. The remaining targets were the Confederates' last major ports, one on the Atlantic and the other on the Gulf. Fort Fisher, commanding the entrance to the Cape Fear River and the port of Wilmington, North Carolina, had to be captured in order to cut off the last trickle of European supplies bound for General Robert E. Lee's beleaguered army. And Mobile Bay had to be wrested from Confederate control to furnish a sheltered harbor for the U.S. Navy's West Gulf Blockading Squadron and clear the way for a large-scale land assault on Mobile itself, 30 miles up the bay.

Mobile Bay was the first of these climactic operations to mature. It had been a long time in coming: The target had been high on Washington's priority list since the early months of the War. An attack seemed to be in the offing in May of 1862, after Flag Officer David Farragut captured New Orleans. But before he could move on Mobile Bay, Farragut was sent north to besiege Vicksburg, a campaign that kept him occupied for more than a year. Finally, in January of 1864, with the entire Mississippi in Federal hands, Farragut — now a rear admiral — arrived off Mobile Bay to mount the operation. And still, he had to mark time for several months while assembling the ships and men he needed for a rigorous campaign.

Mobile Bay presented the admiral with a variety of thorny problems. Though the bay stretched far inland, its entrance was only three miles wide *(map, page 146)*. Fort Gaines, on Dauphin Island, guarded the western side of this entrance; a smaller passage, north of Dauphin Island, was blocked by tiny Fort Powell and impassable obstructions. Stretching eastward from Fort Gaines were a series of sunken pilings that effectively closed more than a mile and a half of the entrance to the bay. Beyond the pilings, the channel was further narrowed by shallow water and submerged mines, or torpedoes — scores of beer kegs and tin cones filled with explosives and fitted with either tubes of fulminate or percussion caps, which would detonate the charge when struck by a ship's hull.

The eastern edge of the mine field was marked by a red buoy that warned blockade runners to hug Mobile Point, 200 yards away. Here was a narrow opening for Farragut. But on Mobile Point, looming above the constricted passageway, stood Fort Morgan. The fort, commanded by Brigadier General Richard L. Page, a cousin of Robert E. Lee, was a massive red-brick pentagon whose three tiers boasted 40 guns, some of them large enough to blast gaping holes in the sides of Farragut's wooden ships. In addition, seven big cannon were emplaced at water level. An invading fleet would have to pass directly under the bastion's guns. Yet Farragut planned to run this gantlet into the bay, where a Confederate flotilla was known to be lurking. After destroying the

Confederate ships, he would turn back and force the forts to surrender by bombardment and siege.

Farragut had delayed his attack largely out of concern for one particularly dangerous Confederate vessel. A shipyard at Selma, 150 miles up the Alabama River from Mobile, had recently built a huge ironclad ram, the 209-foot-long *Tennessee*, and sent her downstream into Mobile Bay. She was yet another of the Confederate ironclads that were supposed to break the blockade and turn the tide of the war at sea. Like her precursors, the *Tennessee* had several shortcomings. She was slow, hard to maneuver and vulnerable at certain vital points. All the same, she was a

This Colt 1851 Navy-model revolver belonged to 20-year-old U.S. Navy Lieutenant Benjamin Porter, who led a detachment of sailors in the vanguard of a land assault on Fort Fisher, North Carolina, in January 1865. Porter lost his life in the attack.

powerful vessel and a daunting threat to Farragut's wooden fleet.

The *Tennessee's* casemate, which housed her crew and six big Brooke rifles, was 79 feet long and 29 feet wide; it was made of thick oak and pine, and armored with three layers of tough, malleable iron bolted together. The iron plating, like the eaves of a house, extended outward and downward before curving inward to meet the hull again four feet below the water line. The hollow thus created was filled with more timber, making the vessel almost invulnerable amidships.

The *Tennessee* had another asset that made her doubly dangerous. This was her captain, Admiral Franklin Buchanan, who also commanded the three wooden gunboats — the *Morgan*, the *Gaines* and the *Selma* — assigned to defend the bay. At the age of 64, Buchan-

an was a year older than Farragut and every bit as aggressive. He had proved his mettle as captain of the ironclad *Merrimac* when she wreaked havoc in Hampton Roads and fought the *Monitor* to a standstill. "Old Buck," as Farragut called his long-time associate in the prewar Navy, was widely considered a master at handling ironclads, and Farragut shared that view. In fact, Buchanan haunted him. Farragut later wrote of his "six months constantly watching day and night for an enemy; to know him to be as brave, as skilful, and as determined as myself; who was pledged to his Government and the South to drive me away and raise the blockade and free the Mississippi from our rule."

To combat Buchanan's *Tennessee* on more equal terms, Farragut had asked the Navy Department to send him several monitors — "damned tea-kettles," he called them. The Navy had promised him four monitors, but they were slow in arriving, and so was the force of 2,000 soldiers that Farragut had called for to "stop up the back door" of his naval assault.

Finally, in July, the monitors began to trickle in. First came the *Manhattan* from the Atlantic Coast, its single turret girded in 10 inches of iron and carrying two 15-inchers. Then the *Chickasaw* arrived from New Orleans, followed the next day by the *Winnebago*, each of them double-turreted with two 11-inchers in each turret. The *Manhattan's* sister ship, the *Tecumseh*, did not make it until August 4, the eve of the battle, and almost got left out. By then, the Army troops under Major General Gordon Granger had been put ashore near Fort Gaines.

According to Farragut's plan of attack, the four monitors would take the lead. Their shallow draft would permit them to travel

The Confederate ironclad *Tennessee* lies at anchor after her capture by the Federals. Two years in the building, the formidable vessel was the flagship of Admiral Franklin Buchanan *(right)*, who earlier had been wounded while commanding the famed *Merrimac* in her duel with the *Monitor* at Hampton Roads.

close to the shore, and their armor and low profiles would protect them from Fort Morgan's guns. The wooden ships would follow slightly behind and to the left of the monitors, using them as a buffer. Farragut had 14 wooden ships in all: eight big screw sloops, a screw steamer and five small gunboats. Because the flotilla would have to pass so close to the fort, each of the smaller and more vulnerable ships was lashed to the port side of a larger one, which would duel Fort Morgan with her starboard broadside. In this symbiotic relationship, the smaller vessels would act as tugs if their consorts' engines were shot up. Once out of range of Fort Morgan's guns, the cables connecting the paired vessels would be cut and each would take its allotted place in the action.

The wooden flotilla would be led by the 24-gun *Brooklyn*, which was equipped with four chase guns on her bow and a mine-sweeping device. To the *Brooklyn* was lashed the gunboat *Octorara*. Following in order would come Farragut's *Hartford* and her mate, the *Metacomet*, then the *Richmond* and the *Port Royal*, the *Lackawanna* and the *Seminole*, the *Monongahela* and the *Kennebec*, the *Ossipee* and the *Itasca*, and finally the *Oneida* and the *Galena*.

As darkness fell on Farragut's fleet on the night of August 4, the officers and crews made final preparations for the attack, then sat down to write letters to their loved ones. Many men were less than optimistic about facing the 47 guns of Fort Morgan while traversing a channel only 200 yards wide, and they wrote with a sense of final leave-taking. Farragut, quietly reverent, placed himself in the hands of his Maker. When an officer suggested that the men be issued a ration of grog to stiffen their resolve, the admiral replied briskly: "No, sir! I never found that I needed rum to enable me to do my duty. I will order two cups of good coffee to each man at two o'clock, and at eight o'clock I will pipe all hands to breakfast in Mobile Bay."

At dawn on August 5, the Federal ships drew up in order of battle. They were stripped of all superfluous spars and rigging in order to achieve maximum speed and maneuverability. Chains had been hung over their sides and sandbags stacked to protect their vital parts. To a Confederate observer, they "appeared like prize fighters ready for the ring."

The Confederates were waiting for the attack. Aboard the *Tennessee*, at anchor near Fort Morgan, Admiral Buchanan was roused from bed at 5:45. He ran on deck to have a look at the advancing Federal fleet. Then he ordered all hands to assemble on the gun

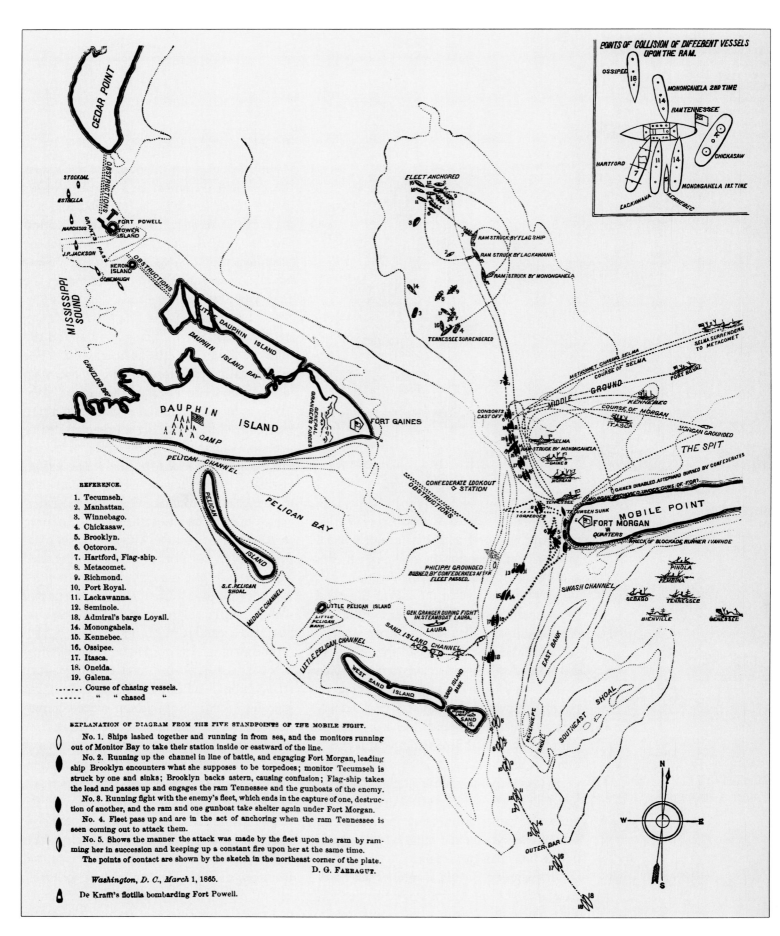

POINTS OF COLLISION OF DIFFERENT VESSELS UPON THE RAM.

OSSIPEE
MONONGAHELA 2ND TIME
RAM TENNESSEE
HARTFORD
CHICKASAW
LACKAWANA
KENNEBEC
MONONGAHELA 1ST TIME

CEDAR POINT

STOCKDAL
ESTELLA
NARCISSUS
J.P. JACKSON
FORT POWELL
TOWER ISLAND
GRANT'S PASS
HERON ISLAND
CONEMAUGH

MISSISSIPPI SOUND

OBSTRUCTIONS

GRAVELINE'S BAY

LITTLE DAUPHIN ISLAND

DAUPHIN ISLAND BAY

DAUPHIN ISLAND

GENERAL GRANGER'S FORCES

CAMP

FORT GAINES

PELICAN CHANNEL

PELICAN ISLAND

PELICAN BAY

S.E. PELICAN SHOAL

MIDDLE CHANNEL

LITTLE PELICAN ISLAND
LITTLE PELICAN BANK

LITTLE PELICAN CHANNEL

SAND ISLAND CHANNEL

WEST SAND ISLAND

SAND ISLAND BANK

SAND IS.

FLEET ANCHORED

RAM STRUCK BY FLAG SHIP
RAM STRUCK BY LACKAWANA
RAM STRUCK BY MONONGAHELA

TENNESSEE SURRENDERED

CONSORTS CAST OFF

SELMA
RAM STRUCK BY MONONGAHELA
GAINES
MORGAN

CONFEDERATE LOOKOUT STATION

OBSTRUCTIONS

TENNESSEE

TORPEDOES

TECUMSEH SUNK

PHILIPPI GROUNDED BURNED BY CONFEDERATES AFTER FLEET PASSED.

GEN. GRANGER DURING FIGHT IN STEAMBOAT LAURA.
LAURA

METACOMET CHASING SELMA
COURSE OF SELMA
PORT ROYAL
SELMA SURRENDERS TO METACOMET

MIDDLE GROUND

KENNEBEC
COURSE OF MORGAN
ITASCA
MORGAN GROUNDED
THE SPIT

GAINES DISABLED. AFTERWARD BURNED BY CONFEDERATES

MORGAN ANCHORED UNDER GUNS OF FORT

MOBILE POINT
FORT MORGAN
QUARTERS

WRECK OF BLOCKADE RUNNER IVANHOE

SWASH CHANNEL

PINOLA
PEMBINA
SEBAGO
TENNESSEE
BIENVILLE
GENESSEE

EAST BANK

REVENUE CT.
EAGLE
SOUTHEAST SHOAL

OUTER BAR

REFERENCE.

1. Tecumseh.
2. Manhattan.
3. Winnebago.
4. Chickasaw.
5. Brooklyn.
6. Octorora.
7. Hartford, Flag-ship.
8. Metacomet.
9. Richmond.
10. Port Royal.
11. Lackawanna.
12. Seminole.
13. Admiral's barge Loyall.
14. Monongahela.
15. Kennebec.
16. Ossipee.
17. Itasca.
18. Oneida.
19. Galena.
...... Course of chasing vessels.
------ " " chased "

EXPLANATION OF DIAGRAM FROM THE FIVE STANDPOINTS OF THE MOBILE FIGHT.

No. 1. Ships lashed together and running in from sea, and the monitors running out of Monitor Bay to take their station inside or eastward of the line.

No. 2. Running up the channel in line of battle, and engaging Fort Morgan, leading ship Brooklyn encounters what she supposes to be torpedoes; monitor Tecumseh is struck by one and sinks; Brooklyn backs astern, causing confusion; Flag-ship takes the lead and passes up and engages the ram Tennessee and the gunboats of the enemy.

No. 3. Running fight with the enemy's fleet, which ends in the capture of one, destruction of another, and the ram and one gunboat take shelter again under Fort Morgan.

No. 4. Fleet pass up and are in the act of anchoring when the ram Tennessee is seen coming out to attack them.

No. 5. Shows the manner the attack was made by the fleet upon the ram by ramming her in succession and keeping up a constant fire upon her at the same time.

The points of contact are shown by the sketch in the northeast corner of the plate.

D. G. FARRAGUT.

Washington, D. C., March 1, 1865.

De Krafft's flotilla bombarding Fort Powell.

1865 U.S. Navy diagram of the
ttle of Mobile Bay shows how the
ips of the Federal fleet moved
tandem up the main channel under
e from Fort Morgan, entered
e torpedo field and emerged into
e bay itself to engage the small
nfederate fleet. To the west,
allower entrances to the bay were
arded by Forts Gaines and Powell.

deck, where he began a short speech: "Now, men, the enemy is coming, and I want you to do your duty." He closed with the injunction: "If I fall, lay me on the side and go on with the fight."

At 6:45, the lead monitor *Tecumseh* fired one of her 15-inchers toward Fort Morgan to test the range. By 7:15, Farragut's ships were steaming into the narrow passage, and the firing had grown intense. Fort Morgan's guns were pounding away at the flotilla, and Farragut's broadsides were punishing the fort.

At this critical time, the Federals found themselves on the brink of disaster. The sluggish monitors, making only a few knots, were being overtaken by the faster wooden ships. The *Brooklyn* stopped short to avoid passing the ironclads. Her captain, James Alden, had no desire to face the *Tennessee* without their protection. The *Hartford* and the other ships behind were forced to slow precipitously to avoid collision.

But to halt was even more dangerous, for the ships were piling up directly under Fort Morgan's guns. Captain Alden sent the *Hartford* an obvious signal: "The monitors are right ahead; we cannot go on without passing them." In exasperation Farragut signaled back, "Order the monitors ahead and go on." But the *Brooklyn* did not move; worse, she drifted broadside across the channel, blocking the way.

Up ahead, Captain Tunis Craven of the monitor *Tecumseh* had a problem of his own: He feared that his awkward ship was going to run aground on the turbulent shoals directly under Fort Morgan. Looking to the deep channel beyond the red buoy, Craven decided to maneuver his ship through the torpedoes. Remarking to his pilot, "It is impos-

sible that the admiral means us to go inside that buoy," he ordered the *Tecumseh* to bear hard aport.

Moments after the ship entered the danger area, her vulnerable underbelly struck a torpedo. She went down swiftly. "Her stern lifted high in the air with the propeller still revolving," wrote an engineer, "and the ship pitched out of sight like an arrow twanged from the bow."

Some of the crewmen scrambled up the ladder to the escape hatch and got out of the sinking ship. Captain Craven and his pilot paused at the foot of the ladder. "After you, Pilot," Craven said. The pilot accepted the offer and made his way out, but as he later testified, "there was nothing after me." The captain and all but 21 of the 113-man complement went down with the *Tecumseh*.

Admiral Farragut was watching the battle from a lofty position aboard his flagship. He had been unable to see much from the deck because of the low-hanging pall of smoke from the guns. So, ignoring the danger, he climbed the rigging of the mainmast and stationed himself just below the maintop platform. The *Hartford's* captain, Percival Drayton, sent a man up to lash Farragut safely to the rigging. There, above the battle's din, spyglass in hand, the admiral relayed orders down to the deck.

With the *Brooklyn* stalled and holding up the line, the wooden ships were taking a terrific pounding from both Fort Morgan and the four Confederate vessels just inside the bay. Aboard the *Hartford*, the carnage was appalling. An Army signal officer assigned to the ship later said that the scene was "sickening beyond the power of words to portray. Shot after shot came through the side, mowing down the men, deluging the decks with

Farragut's fleet trades fire with Fort Morgan and three enemy gunboats (*left*), led by the *Tennessee*. At center, the monitor *Tecumseh* founders after striking a min

blood and scattering mangled fragments of humanity so thickly that it was difficult to stand on the deck, so slippery was it. The bodies of the dead were placed in a long row on the port side, while the wounded were sent below." Blood and flesh from the *Hartford* spattered the deck of the *Metacomet*, lashed to the flagship's side.

Farragut watched the gory stalemate with anger and desperation. The *Hartford* was still being blocked by the motionless *Brooklyn*, and unless the *Brooklyn* moved on, he would have to order the ships to follow the *Tecumseh's* course through the mine field. Once more he signaled the *Brooklyn* to proceed. But Captain Alden, shaken by the sudden sinking of the *Tecumseh*, thought he saw mines in his path and began to back water, signaling the flagship, "Torpedoes ahead!"

For a moment Farragut hesitated. He later wrote that he was praying, and "as if in answer a voice commanded, 'Go on!' " Then the admiral yelled a command that was variously reported, but that entered legend as "Damn the torpedoes! Full speed ahead!"

Brushing by the *Brooklyn*, the *Hartford* moved into the mine field with all guns blazing at Fort Morgan. Finally the *Brooklyn* lurched forward behind the flagship, and the rest of the flotilla followed.

The fleet moved on through the mine field, braving fire from both the fort and the enemy vessels in the bay. Sailors below decks on the *Hartford* and the *Richmond* could hear their ships' hulls bumping against torpedoes, but not one of the mines exploded; their primer tubes had probably been corroded by long exposure in salt water. All of Farragut's vessels made it through, though some were badly shot up. The *Oneida*, dead in the water with her boiler knocked out and

her wheel ropes cut, was towed into Mobile Bay by her consort, the *Galena*.

Inside Fort Morgan, General Page was chagrined that the Federals had slipped past his stronghold, but he remained confident that they were entering a trap. And so it seemed. Just as the *Hartford* cleared the narrows, the Confederate flotilla attacked the flagship. Admiral Buchanan headed the *Tennessee* straight for Farragut's flagship.

High above the obscuring smoke of battle, Admiral Farragut follows the action in Mobile Bay while tied to the *Hartford's* rigging to prevent a fall. His lofty perch was extensively publicized. One newspaper, he noted with amusement afterward, had him "lashed up to the mast like a culprit."

But the ironclad was too slow to catch the nimble *Hartford*.

Quickly, Buchanan swerved toward the *Richmond* and the *Brooklyn* as they steamed out of the mine field. The *Tennessee* put two shells into the *Brooklyn's* hull, killing several sailors. The *Richmond* fired three full 11-gun broadsides at the ram, but the rounds that hit simply bounced off the ironclad's thick hide.

Meanwhile, the little Confederate gunboat *Selma* was boldly shadowing the *Hartford* and raking her decks with deadly fire. Lieutenant Commander James E. Jouett of the *Metacomet*, the fastest Federal vessel, requested permission to cut his ship loose from the *Hartford* so that she could attack the *Selma*. Farragut assented, and the *Metacomet* gave chase, her guns belching fire. The *Selma*, outclassed, fled into shallow waters to avoid her pursuer. Aboard the *Metacomet*, a leadsman warned the captain that the ship was entering waters too shallow for her. In reply, Jouett ordered: "Call the man in. He is only intimidating me with his soundings." The *Metacomet* pressed on and overtook the *Selma*. The Federal gunners went to work, blasting the *Selma's* deck, killing eight men and wounding seven. Then the Confederate captain raised the white flag.

While the *Metacomet* was cornering her prey, the *Tennessee* was working her way along the line of Federal ships. She tried to ram several of them, but the clumsy giant kept missing the target. As if in frustration, she put into safe harbor under the guns of Fort Morgan.

By now, most of the paired Federal ships had been uncoupled, and several set off in pursuit of the Confederate gunboats *Morgan* and *Gaines*. The *Morgan* took shelter under the guns of the fort and escaped that night to the city of Mobile. The *Gaines* was less fortunate. She was mortally wounded by a shot through the hull, and her crew scuttled her as they fled.

Farragut, finding himself with no one to fight, anchored the battered *Hartford* four miles up the bay, and most of his fleet came to rest near him. The admiral ordered his men to be fed the breakfast he had promised them the night before; it was just 8:30 a.m., only 30 minutes behind his own schedule. But before they had drunk their coffee, someone shouted, "The ram is coming!"

The return of the *Tennessee* was a bold but foolhardy act. Buchanan had every reason to stay put and meet the Federal fleet with the full backing of the guns of Fort Morgan. Instead, he deliberately took on a whole flotilla, challenging 157 guns with his six. What had prompted this skillful veteran to take such inordinate risks? Perhaps the galling sight of Farragut and his command riding at ease on Buchanan's home waters. Perhaps the lingering theory, persistent though often disproved, that ironclads were invincible. Certainly, hubris was involved. Months before, Buchanan had remarked of the *Tennessee:* "Everybody has taken it into their heads that one ship can whip a dozen, and if the trial is not made, we who are in her are damned for life."

As Farragut watched his admired enemy approach, he said, "I did not think Old Buck was such a fool." For the moment, Buchanan ignored the slow-moving monitors; it was the wooden ships that would have to bear the brunt of the attack. Farragut ordered the iron-prowed *Monongahela* and the swift *Lackawanna* to "run down the ram."

The *Tennessee* attempted to evade the two attackers and close in on the *Hartford*. But

Waterborne Mines to Fight the U.S. Navy

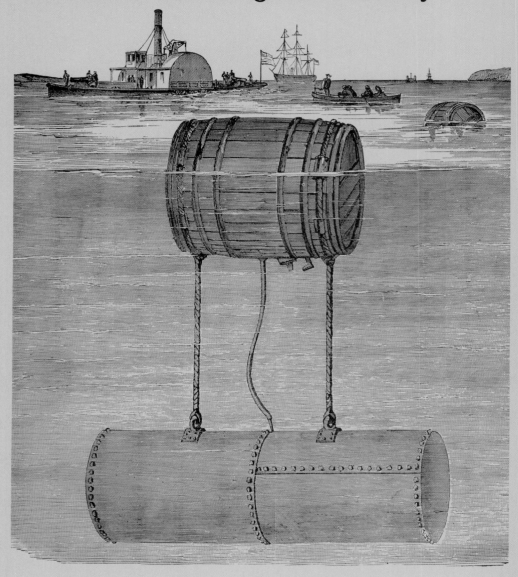

The drift torpedo sketched at left was released in the Potomac River in 1861, but missed its target downstream, the U.S.S. *Wabash*. Before launching this device, the Confederates lit the waterproof fuse leading from the floating barrel to the submerged charge.

This unusual mine was designed to drift against the side of a Federal ship. When the mine stopped moving, a propeller located in its housing would turn in the current, triggering the detonator.

In October of 1862, the Confederate Congress created a new military branch, the Torpedo Service, to wage a novel sort of warfare. The men of this small, select service were responsible for sowing mines in Southern waterways and harbors to defend against Federal warships. They employed torpedoes — as mines were then called — of many sizes and shapes, with encased explosive charges that were detonated by contact with a vessel's hull or by remote control from shore.

The Confederate mines were plagued by faulty detonators and poor waterproofing. Nevertheless, they did a great deal of destructive work throughout Southern waters, sinking or damaging 43 Federal vessels — including four powerful monitors — by the War's end.

The prospect of encountering an enemy torpedo constantly haunted Federal sailors. A U.S. Navy officer wrote: "The knowledge that a simple touch will lay your ship helpless, sinking without even the satisfaction of firing one shot in return, calls for more courage than can be expressed, and a short cruise among torpedoes will sober the most intrepid disposition."

This tin-sheathed mine was supposedly more waterproof than its wooden counterpart *(below)*. It exploded when a ship touched a trigger wire, attached to a nearby float.

The buoyant Rains keg torpedo was the most common Confederate mine. Made from small beer kegs with wooden cones added to each end for stability, it was held just beneath the surface by an anchor.

A spar torpedo, affixed to a long boom on the bow of a Confederate vessel, was the weapon of choice for use against Federal ironclads.

This cone-shaped torpedo made by the Fretwell-Singer company was, like the Rains keg, anchored to float just below the surface. When the mine was struck, a weight inside fell and pulled the trigger.

This drum-shaped mine was fired when its operator, concealed in a pit on the riverbank, pulled a long lanyard. Some mines of the type were fitted with electric detonators connected by wire to shore stations.

The deck of the *Hartford* seethes with action as she grates past the Confederate flagship *Tennessee* and pours on a full broadside. Admiral Farragut stands nonchalantly in the mizzen rigging while the ship's officers watch from the poop deck. In the foreground, a gun crew rushes to reload a Dahlgren.

before she reached her target, the *Mononga-hela* and then the *Lackawanna* smashed at full speed against the ram. The *Monongahe-la's* iron prow was broken off, and she took several shots from the *Tennessee*. The *Lacka-wanna* was also badly damaged in the colli-sion, and as she pulled back, the *Tennessee* sent two shots through her.

The Confederate ship, barely scratched, resumed her slow pursuit of the *Hartford*. This time the two flagships almost met head on; they scraped past each other, port bow to port bow. At point-blank range, the *Hartford* blasted the *Tennessee*. Her solid shot merely dented the ram and then glanced off her bev-eled flank. The ironclad fired back, but be-cause of defective primers only one of her guns discharged. That single shell killed five men and wounded eight aboard the *Hartford*.

By now the entire Federal flotilla was con-verging on the *Tennessee*, pounding her with broadsides, maneuvering for a chance to slam into her. The ram turned this way and that, parrying each blow and inflicting dam-age on each attacker. But always the *Hartford* remained Buchanan's primary target, and al-ways it was Farragut who sought most avidly to deal the Confederate her deathblow.

In one round of their struggle, the *Hart-ford* wheeled in an attempt to strike the *Tennessee* broadside. Instead, the Federal flagship was struck amidships by the *Lacka-wanna* on a ramming run. The blow was tre-mendous, cracking and opening the *Hart-ford's* hull. For a moment it seemed that the flagship would go down, and there were pan-icky shouts of "Save the admiral!" But Far-ragut inspected the damage and was reas-sured to find that the split in the hull began a few inches above the water line. He ordered the *Hartford* to go after the ram once more.

Although the *Tennessee* appeared to be holding her own, the guns of the flotilla were beginning to find the weak spots in her carapace. The ironclad's hull and casemate remained intact, but a Federal round crippled the mechanism that opened and shut the gunports. As a mechanic struggled outside the vessel to open one of the gunports, an 11-inch shell from the monitor *Chickasaw* mashed him to a pulp against the iron. The final blow came when a shell from the *Chickasaw* smashed the *Tennessee's* exposed rudder chain. Now the ram could not be steered.

Aboard the ironclad, Admiral Buchanan learned the bad news secondhand. He was lying in his cabin, racked with pain from a leg broken by a ricocheting bolt. Captain James D. Johnston came down to tell him the ship was totally disabled, and he gritted out an answer through clenched teeth: "Well, Johnston, if you cannot do them any further damage you had better surrender."

Johnston stopped the engine and raised a white flag. The U.S.S. *Ossipee* sent over a small boat to accept the surrender and carry the defeated admiral's sword back to the victor. "The Almighty has smiled upon me once more," Farragut later wrote his wife. "It was a hard fight but Buck met his fate manfully." The *Tennessee* had lost two men killed and nine wounded, bringing the number of Confederate casualties to 32. On the Federal side, 170 men were wounded and 145 were dead, including those who went down in the *Tecumseh*.

With the *Tennessee's* defeat, Farragut's fleet settled in to force the surrender of Forts Gaines and Morgan; tiny Fort Powell had already been evacuated. The two Confederate strongholds resisted, but they were cut off from aid and attacked by 17 warships,

and by Army units reinforced to a strength of 5,500. It was only a matter of time. The garrison at Fort Gaines gave up on August 8. On August 23, the white flag was raised over Fort Morgan. But General Page refused to send his sword to Farragut; he broke it and flung the pieces away. The admiral called Page's defiance "childish spitefulness."

The Federals would not take the city of Mobile until the following April, after a land attack led by Major General E.R.S. Canby forced the Confederates to evacuate the city. But Farragut's success at the entrance to Mobile Bay had an immediate impact. With that victory, the entire Gulf Coast east of the Mississippi was closed to Confederate shipping and blockade runners. Now the only major Confederate seaport left open was Wilmington. To seal it, the Federals would have to conquer a bastion that was widely considered the most strongly fortified position in the world.

Strategists on both sides in the summer of 1864 acknowledged the importance of Fort Fisher, 20 miles down the Cape Fear River from Wilmington. Robert E. Lee sent word to the fort's commander, 29-year-old Colonel William Lamb, that unless his stronghold kept Wilmington open to blockade runners, the Confederacy could not sustain Lee's army in the field. And in Washington, Secretary Welles wrote on August 30: "Something must be done to close the entrance to Cape Fear River and port of Wilmington. I have been urging a conjoint attack for months. Could we seize the forts at the entrance of Cape Fear and close the illicit traffic, it would be almost as important as the capture of Richmond on the fate of the Rebels." Secretary of War Edwin Stanton and

General in Chief Ulysses S. Grant agreed to Welles's proposal for a coordinated assault.

Admiral Farragut was offered command of the flotilla, but he declined on the grounds of exhaustion and poor health. The post fell to Farragut's boastful and ambitious foster brother, David Porter. Although Porter had been appointed acting rear admiral in September 1862, his recent career was less than impressive, featuring a thoroughly undistinguished performance in the Red River Campaign. Nevertheless, Porter was the boldest and most experienced naval commander available. Exercising his right to lead the 6,500 Army troops committed to the assault was the contentious and unreliable Major General Benjamin Butler, now head of the military district in which Fort Fisher was located.

Butler and Porter were a perfect mismatch; they had cordially disliked each other since the capture of New Orleans. Butler had

Gaping holes in the brick lighthouse near Fort Morgan give evidence of the withering fire that the fort and its environs took from the Federal forces during the battle for Mobile Bay. Even the guns of the captured *Tennessee* were turned against the Confederate strongpoint.

started it all by asserting tactlessly, though with considerable justification, that Porter's mortar boat bombardment of the two forts below the city had made no contribution to the surrender of those strongholds, which had given up the fight after New Orleans fell. Now the admiral and the general communicated with each other mainly through intermediaries — a state of affairs that could easily lead to disaster in a campaign.

Of all the Confederate ports, Wilmington had been the most difficult to blockade. This was largely because the Cape Fear River had two entrances: New Inlet, north of Smith's Island, and the Western Bar Channel, west of the island. Thus the Federals had to keep on duty two flotillas, requiring almost twice as many ships as the 20 needed to close off Charleston. Even so, the blockade was ineffective. In the last nine weeks of 1864 and the first two weeks of 1865, blockade runners docked in Wilmington with 69,000 rifles, 43 cannon, more than four tons of meat, a half million pairs of shoes, about a ton of saltpeter and three quarters of a ton of lead.

The two entrances to the river were dominated from the mainland by Forts Caswell and Fisher, the former guarding the Western Bar Channel and the latter perched on a bluff overlooking the entrance to New Inlet. Fort Fisher had earthen walls, bolstered with heavy timbers and covered with sod; these ramparts were 25 feet thick at the base, tapering to eight feet at the top, and they averaged 20 feet in height. The fort's sea face ran north for more than a mile, then the walls turned west at a right angle and extended almost a half mile overland, nearly reaching the Cape Fear River. In front of this land face, the defenders had constructed a wooden palisade and seeded the ground with hundreds of mines as protection against an infantry assault from the north.

The fort boasted 169 artillery pieces, of which 44 were heavy cannon. Separating the gun platforms were 30 thick, mound-like earthen traverses, 15 feet higher than the parapet; if a direct hit destroyed one platform, the adjoining ones would be sheltered by these traverses, some of which were hollowed out to serve as bombproofs and powder magazines.

At the southern end of the sea face was the cone-shaped Mound Battery, rising 60 feet above the beach, with its two big guns bearing on New Inlet. A mile farther south, a separate bastion, Battery Buchanan, guarded the tip of Confederate Point (formerly named Federal Point). David Porter, for once, did not overstate the challenge he was facing when he claimed that only one who had seen Fort Fisher "could form the slightest conception of these works — their magnitude, strength and extent." But if U.S. Army and Navy forces working together could somehow reduce this stronghold, the much less formidable Fort Caswell would certainly fall, isolating Wilmington.

Benjamin Butler came up with a peculiar plan for taking Fort Fisher — one that would do nothing to restore his declining reputation among his fellow commanders. The general, always excited by flamboyant novelties, had been fascinated by accounts of two ship explosions: A British canal boat had blown up with 75 tons of powder in its hold and, more recently, a U.S. ordnance vessel had exploded at City Point, east of Richmond. Both blasts had destroyed buildings in the vicinity and caused great loss of life. Butler concluded that an old ship filled with explosives and set off beneath Fisher

The two faces of L-shaped Fort Fisher, in red, guard the approach to the Cape Fear River. The land face *(top)* stretched 682 yards between the river and the Atlantic Ocean, mounting 20 guns between protective, earthen traverses. The 24-gun sea face ran parallel to the beach for 1,898 yards and ended at the towering Mound Battery.

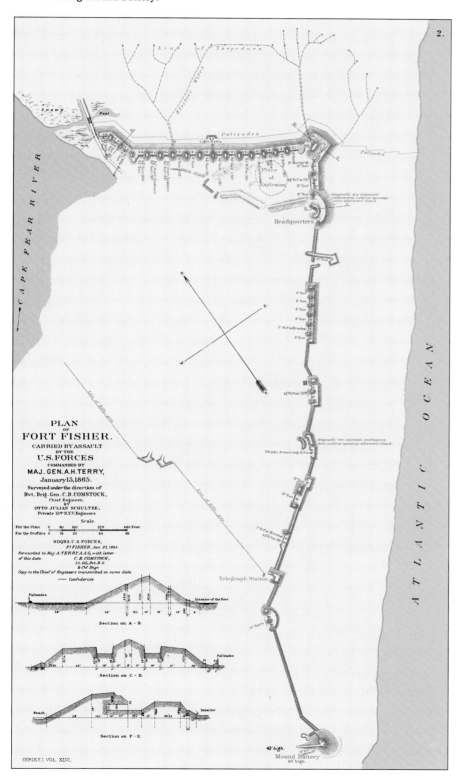

PLAN
OF
FORT FISHER.
CARRIED BY ASSAULT
BY THE
U.S. FORCES
COMMANDED BY
MAJ. GEN. A.H. TERRY,
January 15, 1865.
Surveyed under the direction of
Bvt. Brig. Gen. C.B. COMSTOCK,
Chief Engineer,
BY
OTTO JULIAN SCHULTZE,
Private 13th N.Y. Engineers.
Scale.

CAPE FEAR RIVER

ATLANTIC OCEAN

would have a similar effect — at the very least, opening the walls of the fort to an infantry assault.

To everyone's surprise, Porter, who was known to disdain ideas that he did not originate, agreed that Butler's notion was an "experiment at least worth trying." So an ancient, flat-bottomed derelict named the *Louisiana* was filled to the gunwales with 215 tons of powder and assorted combustibles. This immense floating bomb was to be towed into the shallows off Fort Fisher, and there she would wreak magnificent destruction.

On December 15, Butler and his Army transports arrived off New Inlet. The weather was clear, the sea calm, the temperature balmy — perfect conditions for a landing. But the Navy was nowhere to be seen: an unpromising start for an amphibious operation. Fully three days passed before Porter hove in sight. He came with a flotilla even mightier than the one Farragut had brought to New Orleans. There were 150 ships, including the vaunted ironclad *New Ironsides*, and they mounted nearly 600 guns.

But by now the weather had turned ominous, and Porter advised Butler to take his transports back to Beaufort, North Carolina, 75 miles to the north, to await more favorable conditions. Five days later, when the sea was placid once more, Butler sent word that he and his men would return to the rendezvous point the next night, Christmas Eve, ready to swarm ashore as soon as the Navy opened the way for them.

Porter, however, having warmed to Butler's bombship idea, now saw little need to postpone its execution until the Army arrived. He told a fellow officer that when the *Louisiana* blew, "houses in Wilmington will tumble to the ground and much demoralize

the people, and I think if the rebels fight after the explosion they have more in them than I give them credit for." The night before Butler and his troops were due to arrive, Porter ordered the U.S.S. *Wilderness*, manned by Commander Alexander C. Rhind and a skeleton crew, to tow the *Louisiana* to within 500 yards of the beach just north of the fort. The two ships ran through the Stygian night without lights and arrived undetected. Crewmen rowed to the bombship,

where they set clockwork detonators to trigger the explosion at 1:20 a.m.; for good measure, they lit a pine fire in a stack of wood in the after cabin. Then they hastily rowed back to the *Wilderness*.

Porter, expecting a cataclysmic explosion, had ordered his vessels to stand 12 miles offshore. From there he watched through his telescope in eager anticipation. But the moment for the ultimate explosion came and went in deathly silence. The detonators had

Bursting shells rip through Confederate gun crews manning the Mound Battery at the tip of Fort Fisher's sea face. Extending northward, a string of guns protected by 30-foot-high sand traverses duel with the ships of Admiral David Porter's Federal fleet offshore.

failed. Now it was left to the wood fire to set off the blast. And it did. At 1:40 a.m., the *Louisiana* blew up.

But the explosion was a terrible disappointment — not a stupendous roar but a discreet rumble, like the low boom "produced by the discharge of a 100-pounder," wrote a *New York Times* reporter with the fleet. Unfortunately for Porter, about 80 per cent of the powder was defective and failed to detonate. An impressive tongue of flame did arise. It quickly turned into a black cloud of dust and smoke that was carried out to sea by the wind. Sniffing the great cloud as it wafted past the anchored fleet, a second reporter said it resembled "a monstrous waterspout filling the atmosphere with its sulphurous odor, as if a spirit from the infernal regions had swept by us." Tremors were experienced at Fort Fisher and much farther away. But the bastion's great earthworks were undamaged.

Porter was unfazed. He decided to press forward with the naval attack, and by 11:30 that morning he had deployed his fleet in a semicircle along the fort's sea face. The ships began their bombardment and for five hours hit the fort with everything they had, firing about 10,000 rounds. It was the start of the War's heaviest naval bombardment to date, totaling 21,000 rounds by the end of the second day. But the range was too long for accuracy, and little damage was done to Fort Fisher's works. The lesson taught at Charleston — that a well-constructed earthen fort could not be leveled by cannon — had yet to be fully absorbed. Only two of the stronghold's guns were knocked off their carriages, and the 23 Confederate casualties were less than half the number suffered by the Federals, even though the fort's garri-son, trying to conserve ammunition, fired only 672 rounds.

At dusk, General Butler arrived off Confederate Point with a few transports and blandly explained to Porter that the rest of his force would be arriving the next day. The admiral ordered a cease fire, insisting that no further bombardment would be necessary. The fort was virtually silenced, he claimed; all the Army had to do was walk in and take possession. Porter was eventually persuaded to contribute some shells to cover the next morning's landing.

At 10:30 a.m. on Christmas Day, the fleet renewed its bombardment, and three hours later about 2,000 troops under Major General Godfrey Weitzel, second in command to Butler, came ashore above Fort Fisher and began moving south toward the land face. Weitzel doubted Porter's boasts that the fort was close to surrender, and his skepticism was well-founded. His men were greeted by intermittent artillery and musket fire. In fact, all 17 cannon on the fort's land face were unharmed; their gun crews had merely taken cover in the nearby bombproofs. A daring Federal officer, Lieutenant William H. Walling, sprinted across the mine field, scrambled up the parapet and snatched a Confederate flag from atop the earthworks, returning with it to his lines. But his gallant sally, which later won him the Congressional Medal of Honor, changed nothing.

Pickets taken prisoner by the Federals during the advance told Weitzel that Confederate General Robert Hoke, with 6,000 reinforcements, had arrived at Wilmington by train and would soon be moving on his rear. This new threat prompted Butler to decide unilaterally to stop the attack. On his orders, the men in blue turned their backs on

161

Fort Fisher at 6 p.m. and withdrew to the beach, where their small boats waited in the pounding surf.

Butler signaled Porter his decision and turned his transports north toward Virginia and the safety of Hampton Roads. About 700 Federal soldiers were left behind in the hasty retreat, and all during the next day and into the morning of the 27th, Porter covered "those poor devils," as he called the abandoned soldiers, with an umbrella of fire until they could be evacuated. By then the fleet had lobbed so many shells into the fort that a Confederate lieutenant testified that anyone inspecting the works could "walk on nothing but iron."

The admiral had cause to be furious with the general. Butler had demanded so little of his attackers that they had sustained just 16 casualties, including one death by drowning. Gradually, so as not to give the impression that he had been repulsed, Porter sent his ships to Beaufort to be refitted and take on more ammunition. "If this temporary failure succeeds in sending General Butler into private life, it is not to be regretted," he wrote to Secretary Welles. General Grant, agreeing that the expedition was "a gross and culpable failure," wired Porter to stay put in Beaufort, "and I will endeavor to be back again with an increased force and without the former commander."

Though Butler had often been attacked for his military shortcomings, his many friends and allies always had saved him. But this time, men in high places were no longer willing to rally round him. His retreat brought an end to his military career: He was instructed to report home to Massachusetts to await reassignment. Instead, he made his way to Washington, there to plead his case

Colonel William Lamb, commander of Fort Fisher, was a newspaper editor in Norfolk, Virginia, before the War. Severely wounded in the final assault on the fort, he spent seven years on crutches.

in vain among his disillusioned supporters.

The first attack on Fort Fisher had ended. Jubilantly, Colonel Lamb wired his superiors in Richmond: "This morning, December 27, the foiled and frightened enemy left our shore." But a second and more determined Federal attack would soon begin.

In the course of the failed campaign, the strategic picture had changed for the Federal cause. Major General William Tecumseh Sherman had taken Savannah and was ranging north through the Carolinas, capturing or demolishing objectives at will. Wilmington now became a prospective supply depot for Sherman's army. Its capture was imperative, and Grant was prepared to devote to the effort whatever manpower and matériel were required.

Major General Alfred Howe Terry, who led the Army's attack on Fort Fisher, sits amid his staff beneath the flag of X Corps, which he commanded in 1864. His brother Adrian (far left) was his chief of staff. Terry, often regarded as the best volunteer officer to emerge from the War, received an expression of gratitude from Congress for his role at Fort Fisher.

On January 8, 1865, more than 8,000 Federal troops, many of them veterans of the Butler expedition, embarked from Bermuda Hundred on the James River, bound for a second strike at Fort Fisher. To replace Butler as commander of the Army's contingent, Grant appointed 37-year-old Major General Alfred H. Terry, who had served in the previous assault and had earlier distinguished himself on Morris Island during the attack on Charleston. Trained as a lawyer at Yale, Terry was one of those rare volunteer officers who, by innate ability, rose through the ranks to high command. He was experienced in Army-Navy operations and had the equanimity to work closely with Porter without rubbing the temperamental admiral the wrong way. The two leaders would plan every detail of the coming attack in harmony.

At Fort Fisher, Colonel Lamb's men quickly repaired the damage of the first attack. But Lamb's superior—the stubborn, irascible General Braxton Bragg—refused to send reinforcements from Hoke's nearby division, feeling that he needed those 6,000 troops to defend Wilmington. Besides, Bragg believed that there would not be another seaborne assault soon. Thus, when

the massive Federal fleet appeared with the Army transports off Confederate Point on January 12, 1865, Lamb's fortifications were manned by only 700 to 800 men.

On the following morning, just after dawn, Porter's flotilla opened fire. During the first day's action, Lamb did receive modest reinforcements, bringing his total force to about 1,500 men. Also joining him was the district commander, Major General W.H.C. Whiting, a talented military engineer who had spent the better part of two years in planning and building the intricate fort. Whiting found Lamb directing the defense from one of its ramparts. "Lamb, my boy," the general said, "I have come to share your fate. You and your garrison are to be sacrificed." Appalled, Lamb replied, "Don't say so, General; we shall certainly whip the enemy again." Whiting had no intention of giving up, but he was embittered by Bragg's unwillingness to send Hoke's force. As late as the afternoon of the 15th, Bragg would assure General Lee that the Federals were bound to fail because the fort had not been surrounded — and could not be unless or until the Federal fleet forced its way into the Cape Fear River.

In contrast to Porter's wild cannonading during his December attack on Fort Fisher, the admiral's fire this time, as Lamb observed, "was concentrated, and the defined object of the fleet was the destruction of the land defenses by enfilade and direct fire." Each squadron of the fleet took up its assigned bombardment station, and each ship aimed at a specific target. The frailer and smaller vessels were to supply the warships with additional ammunition or bring in coal from Beaufort.

Suffering under the Federals' heavy and accurate fire, Colonel Lamb and his men were hard-pressed to carry on. "All day and night on the 13th and 14th of January," Lamb recorded, "the navy continued its ceaseless torment; it was impossible to repair damages at night on the land-face. The *Ironsides* and monitors bowled their 11 and 15 inch shells along the parapet, scattering shrapnel in the darkness. We could scarcely gather up and bury our dead without fresh casualties. At least 200 had been killed and wounded in the two days since the fight began. Only three or four of my land guns were of any service." Bragg had finally responded to Whiting's desperate pleas for reinforcements. But only 350 of the 1,100 troops he dispatched reached the fort; the remainder were forced to turn back by Porter's fire.

Meanwhile, General Terry's troops had entered the fray. Beginning at about 8 a.m. on January 13, some 200 small boats hauled by tugs had brought ashore 8,000 men on the beach five miles north of Fort Fisher. Each soldier carried 40 rounds and rations for three days. But Terry was determined to capture the fort whether it took three days or two weeks. Indeed, his first act ashore was to order defensive works dug across the half-mile-wide peninsula, to be manned by a large part of his command — two brigades of United States Colored Troops under Brigadier General Charles J. Paine. This force was to guard against any attack from Confederates to the north. Unknown to Terry, Hoke was also assuming a defensive position on orders from Bragg.

On the morning of the 14th, a Federal column was sent out to probe the land face of the fort. Taking the lead himself, Terry moved up to within 700 yards of the parapet, made a quick survey of the territory and decided to launch a full-scale assault the

Dr. Jonas W. Lyman, photographed with his daughter Libbie, resigned as surgeon of the 57th Pennsylvania in 1864 in order to join the 203rd Pennsylvania as a lieutenant colonel. In the battle for Fort Fisher, he was shot through the heart while leading his new regiment in an assault on the fifth traverse.

next day. That evening he repaired to Porter's flagship, where the two commanders planned their joint attack.

Besides Paine's two brigades and a reserve brigade, Terry had 3,300 troops available to storm the fort's land face — a division of three brigades commanded by a talented young West Pointer, Brigadier General Adelbert Ames. Porter, always eager to win glory for the Navy, suggested that a contingent of 1,600 sailors and 400 Marines, led by Lieutenant Commander K. R. Breese, simultaneously charge the fort at the so-called Crescent Battery, where the land and sea faces met.

The scheme was a bit harebrained: Sailors fighting on land were always an unknown quantity. But Porter persuaded Terry that his tars were equal to the task; they would advance in three columns, scale the fort's steep parapet and engage the enemy hand to hand with cutlasses and revolvers even as General Ames and his infantrymen were carrying out a similar operation to the west.

Porter assembled a volunteer force and instructed them to "board the fort on the run in a seaman-like way." To the Navy Department and some of his subordinate officers, the admiral confidently suggested that if the Army failed again, he would take Fort Fisher with his own bluejackets.

The sailors and Marines managed to land and dig protective rifle pits without being observed from the fort, most of whose defenders were in the bombproofs seeking shelter from the fleet's relentless cannonading. The Navy men under Commander Breese were to charge when all the guns on the ships suddenly fell silent at 2 p.m. Once the attacking columns had scaled the parapet, Porter's guns would commence firing again, but only on the sea face, where no Federal troops would be engaged.

The sailors waited anxiously for the silence that would be their attack signal. But the time came, and the ships were still firing. Breese was hard put to keep his men in order. The Marines, who were supposed to bring up the rear, providing backup fire with their muskets, suddenly pulled back toward the beach; their trenches were needed by Ames's infantry, and they were trying to reestablish themselves in a safe shelf on the oceanfront. But some of the sailors, seeing the Marines pass to their rear, assumed that a retreat had begun and trotted after them.

At 2:30 p.m., the silence that signaled the attack finally settled over the fleet. "Charge! Charge!" shouted an officer onshore. Sailors

and Marines rushed forward, yelling and cheering — not in three waves according to plan, but in a jumbled mass to which no orders could be passed.

By this time, a Confederate sentinel, Private Arthur Muldoon, had spotted the hectic assault and spread the alarm. Immediately, Confederate infantrymen rushed to the parapet, urged on by General Whiting. A Federal soldier reported: "One Rebel officer stood up there clapping his hands, singing out to his men to kill the Yankee sons of bitches." To support the guns that had not been dismounted from the fort's land face, Colonel Lamb brought up all the small artillery that could be moved, and soon the bluejackets were being showered with grapeshot and canister. U.S. Lieutenant Commander Thomas A. Selfridge Jr. wrote of his men, "They were packed like sheep in a pen, while the enemy were crowding the ramparts not 40 yards away and shooting into them as fast as they could fire."

The Navy men, totally untrained for fighting on land, turned and fled, leaving 300 of their comrades dead or wounded on the beach. Some of the wounded would drown in the incoming tide.

A cry of triumph went up from the defenders. But suddenly Lamb caught sight of three Union flags fluttering from the fort's western salient. He had thought the invaders were repelled, but a larger and better-prepared force — General Ames's division — had gained a footing at the other end of the land face.

Ames and his troops had had their troubles. While they were waiting on a road by the Cape Fear River for the attack to begin, the Confederate gunboat *Chickamauga* had spotted them from the river and fired into

167

their ranks. The soldiers were forced to take cover among the scrub trees and sand hills. Once they had formed up again, they were late for their scheduled assault on the fort; they attacked after the Navy men did. As Admiral Porter was quick to point out afterward, these mischances may have been fortunate, for the Confederates were distracted from the main attack and persuaded to concentrate their artillery in the east angle. In response, Ames's three brigades swept one after the other toward the less heavily fortified western salient. Soon they merged chaotically into a cheering mass crowned with glistening bayonets. They burst through the palisade in the teeth of cannon fire, scaled the parapet and fought the Confederates in vicious hand-to-hand battles from one gun emplacement to the next.

The conquest of the three westernmost traverses and the guns around them cost the Federals dearly. A round of canister cut down the entire color guard of the 97th Pennsylvania. All three brigade commanders—Colonels Newton M. Curtis, Galusha Pennypacker and Louis Bell—were severely wounded, Bell mortally. (Both Curtis and Pennypacker would be appointed brigadier generals for their actions that day, making the 20-year-old Pennypacker the youngest general in the Federal Army.)

The fighting then shifted eastward to the fourth traverse, where Colonel John W. Moore of the 203rd Pennsylvania was killed as he led his men forward waving the regimental flag. At the fifth traverse, Lieutenant Colonel Jonas Lyman of the 203rd killed a Confederate in hand-to-hand combat, only to be shot dead a moment later.

The Confederates also lost some prominent officers in the struggle. General Whit-

Federal soldiers take possession of Fort Fisher's command post, known as the Pulpit Battery. Originally a six-gun emplacement on the fort's sea face, its gun embrasures had been sealed and its roomy bombproof converted into headquarters for Colonel Lamb and his staff.

ing, among the first to reach the contested western salient, was confronted by a score of Federals demanding his surrender; he refused, and they shot him down. Colonel Lamb, who arrived on the scene soon after with the main body of defenders, fought long and hard to stem the Federal tide. He even rounded up wounded men from the fort's improvised hospital and led them back into the fight. But he too fell, severely wounded in the hip, as he led a final desperate charge.

During this struggle for the northern wall of the fort, Admiral Porter's gunners, under his personal direction, performed a feat that compensated in some degree for the ill-conceived land attack by his sailors. With astonishing precision, the rifled pivot guns of the *New Ironsides* and several smaller vessels cleared the enemy out of each successive gun platform just ahead of the advancing Federal troops. The gunners were rarely off target, and only a handful of Federal troops were killed or wounded by stray shots. Such sharpshooter accuracy helped the Army take emplacement after emplacement with fewer casualties than they had reason to expect.

Once the land face was in Federal hands, the rest of the stronghold was doomed to fall. Major James Reilly of the 10th North Carolina, next in command to Colonel Lamb, had hoped to hold out in Battery Buchanan to the south, but when he found this last bastion abandoned by its defenders with its guns spiked, he knew the fight was over. At 10 o'clock that night, Reilly strode onto the beach in front of the fort, holding a white flag. As a Federal officer approached, the major said curtly, "We surrender."

That evening, Porter's ships staged a victory celebration: The coast, one observer wrote, was lit by "battle lanterns, calcium lights, magnificent rockets, blue lights and every description of fireworks." There was revelry, too, among the victors in the fort, though many were aghast at the human wreckage of the battle. "If hell is what it is said to be," wrote a Federal sailor, "then the interior of Fort Fisher is a fair comparison. Here and there you see great heaps of human beings laying just as they fell, one upon the other. Some groaning piteously, and asking for water. Others whose mortal career is over, still grasping the weapon they used to so good an effect in life." The battle, one of the War's fiercest fights, had cost the U.S. Army 955 casualties, while 383 Navy men lay dead or wounded. The Confederates had lost about 500 killed or wounded, and well over 1,000 of the fort's defenders had been taken prisoner.

Even as the Federals celebrated their victory, Fort Fisher claimed still more victims. That night a group of New York soldiers bedded down for the night on a soft, comfortable patch of sod that happened to be the roof of the fort's main powder magazine. Around dawn two tipsy sailors, carrying torches and looking for trophies, entered the magazine. Almost at once, tons of gunpowder exploded. When the dust settled, 104 Federals lay dead or injured.

The coastal war was over. From Virginia down to Florida and westward along the Gulf to the Mississippi, not a single important port remained open to sustain the faltering Confederate cause. The larger conflict would be decided not at sea but in inland battles involving great armies. Yet in that final struggle, the Federals would be inestimably aided by the crushing results of their assaults on the Confederates' coastal strongholds.

The devastation in Fort Fisher's second traverse bears witness to the accuracy of Admiral Porter's gunners. "The scene was indescribably horrible," Colonel Lamb later wrote. "Great cannon broken in two, their carriages wrecked, and among the ruins the mutilated bodies of my dead and dying comrades."

ACKNOWLEDGMENTS

The editors thank the following individuals and institutions for their help in the preparation of this volume:

Georgia: Atlanta — Thomas S. Dickey.

Louisiana: New Orleans — Pat McWhorter, Jan White, Michele Wychoff, The Historic New Orleans Collection.

Maryland: Annapolis — Sigrid Trumpy, United States Naval Academy Museum.

Massachusetts: New Bedford — Carl Cruz.

New York: West Point — Robert Fisch, West Point Museum, United States Military Academy.

Ohio: Cleveland — John Grabowski, Charles Sherrill, Western Reserve Historical Society.

Pennsylvania: Carlisle — Michael J. Winey, United States Army Military History Institute. Harrisburg — William C. Davis, Historical Times, Inc.

Virginia: Richmond — Cathy Carlson, David Hahn, Museum of the Confederacy; Rebecca Perrine, Virginia Historical Society; David L. Griffith, Virginia Museum of Fine Arts.

Washington, D.C.: Eveline Nave, Library of Congress, Photoduplication Service; Alan Stypeck, Second Story Books.

The index for this book was prepared by Nicholas J. Anthony.

BIBLIOGRAPHY

Books

Anderson, Bern, *By Sea and by River: The Naval History of the Civil War.* Alfred A. Knopf, 1962.

Andrews, J. Cutler:
The North Reports the Civil War. University of Pittsburgh Press, 1955.
The South Reports the Civil War. Princeton University Press, 1970.

Barnes, John Sanford, *Submarine Warfare, Offensive and Defensive, Including a Discussion of the Offensive Torpedo System.* Van Nostrand, 1869.

Barrett, John Gilchrist:
The Civil War in North Carolina. The University of North Carolina Press, 1963.
North Carolina as a Civil War Battleground, 1861-1865. North Carolina Department of Cultural Resources, 1980.

Berlin, Ira, ed., *Freedom: A Documentary History of Emancipation, 1861-1867* (Series 2, *The Black Military Experience*). Cambridge University Press, 1982.

Brandt, J. D., *Gunnery Catechism, as Applied to the Service of Naval Ordnance.* Van Nostrand, 1865.

Bridges, Hal, *Lee's Maverick General: Daniel Harvey Hill.* McGraw-Hill Book Company, Inc., 1961.

Burchard, Peter, *One Gallant Rush: Robert Gould Shaw and His Brave Black Regiment.* St. Martin's Press, 1965.

Burns, Zed H., *Confederate Forts.* Southern Historical Publications, Inc., 1977.

Burton, E. Milby, *The Siege of Charleston, 1861-1865.* The University of South Carolina Press, 1970.

Canfield, Eugene B., *Civil War Naval Ordnance.* U.S. Government Printing Office, 1969.

Catton, Bruce:
Mr. Lincoln's Army. Doubleday & Company, Inc., 1951.
Never Call Retreat (*The Centennial History of the Civil War*, Vol. 3). Doubleday & Company, Inc., 1965.

Clark, Harvey, *My Experience with Burnside's Expedition and 18th Army Corps.* Gardner, 1914.

Clark, Walter, ed., *Histories of the Several Regiments and Battalions from North Carolina in the Great War, 1861-'65,* Vols. 1-5. Broadfoot's Bookmark, 1982.

Conway's All the World's Fighting Ships, 1860-1905. Conway Maritime Press Ltd., 1979.

Copp, Elbridge J., *Reminiscences of the War of the Rebellion, 1861-1865.* Elbridge J. Copp, 1911.

Crozier, Emmet, *Yankee Reporters, 1861-65.* Oxford University Press, 1956.

Davis, William C., ed., *The Guns of '62* (*The Image of War, 1861-1865,* Vol. 2). Doubleday & Company, Inc., 1982.

Derby, W. P., *Bearing Arms in the Twenty-Seventh Massachusetts Regiment of Volunteer Infantry during the Civil War, 1861-1865.* Wright & Potter Printing Company, 1883.

Dickey, Thomas S., and Peter C. George, *Field Artillery Projectiles of the American Civil War.* Arsenal Press, 1980.

Drake, J. Madison, *The History of the Ninth New Jersey Veteran Vols.* Journal Printing House, 1889.

Du Pont, H. A., *Rear-Admiral Samuel Francis Du Pont.* National Americana Society, 1926.

Eldredge, D., *The Third New Hampshire and All about It.* Press of E. B. Stillings and Company, 1893.

Emilio, Luis F., *History of the Fifty-Fourth Regiment of Massachusetts Volunteer Infantry, 1863-1865.* The Boston Book Company, 1894.

Foote, Shelby:
The Civil War, a Narrative: Fort Sumter to Perryville. Random House, 1958.
The Civil War, a Narrative: Fredericksburg to Meridian. Random House, 1963.

Foster, John Y., *New Jersey and the Rebellion.* Martin R. Dennis & Co., 1868.

Fox, Gustavus Vasa, *Confidential Correspondence of Gustavus Vasa Fox,* Vols. 1 and 2. Ed. by Robert Means Thompson and Richard Wainwright. Books for Libraries Press, 1972.

Freeman, Douglas Southall, *Lee's Lieutenants: A Study in Command,* Vols. 1-3. Charles Scribner's Sons, 1942-1944.

Hubbard, Charles Eustis, *The Campaign of the Forty-Fifth Regiment, Massachusetts Volunteer Militia.* The "Company A Associates" of the Forty-Fifth Regiment, M.V.M., 1882.

Johnson, John, *The Defense of Charleston Harbor, Including Fort Sumter and the Adjacent Islands, 1863-1865.* Books for Libraries Press, 1970.

Johnson, Robert Underwood, and Clarence Clough Buel, eds., *Battles and Leaders of the Civil War,* Vols. 1, 2 and 4. Castle Books, 1956.

Jones, Samuel, *The Siege of Charleston: And the Operations on the South Atlantic Coast in the War among the States.* The Neale Publishing Company, 1911.

Jones, Virgil Carrington, *The Final Effort* (*The Civil War at Sea,* Vol. 3). Holt, Rinehart and Winston, 1962.

Lamb, William, *Colonel Lamb's Story of Fort Fisher: The Battles Fought Here in 1864 and 1865.* The Blockade Runner Museum, 1966.

Macartney, Clarence Edward, *Mr. Lincoln's Admirals.* Funk & Wagnalls Company, 1956.

McDonough, James L., *Schofield: Union General in the Civil War and Reconstruction.* Florida State University Press, 1972.

Mahan, A. T.:
Admiral Farragut. Greenwood Press, Publishers, 1968.
The Gulf and Inland Waters. Jack Brussel, Publisher, no date.

Mann, Albert W., *History of the Forty-Fifth Regiment: Massachusetts Volunteer Militia.* Brookside Print, 1908.

Mende, Elsie Porter, *An American Soldier and Diplomat: Horace Porter.* Frederick A. Stokes Company, 1927.

Merrill, James M., *Battle Flags South: The Story of the Civil War Navies on Western Waters.* Fairleigh Dickinson University Press, 1970.

Nash, Howard P., Jr., *A Naval History of the Civil War.* A. S. Barnes and Company, Inc., 1972.

Nevins, Allan:
The Organized War, 1863-1864 (*The War for the Union*, Vol. 3). Charles Scribner's Sons, 1971.
War Becomes Revolution, 1862-1863 (*The War for the Union,* Vol. 2). Charles Scribner's Sons, 1960.

Niven, John, *Gideon Welles: Lincoln's Secretary of the Navy.* Oxford University Press, 1973.

Palmer, Abraham J., *The History of the Forty-Eighth Regiment, New York State Volunteers, in the War for the Union.* The Veteran Association of the Regiment, 1885.

Parton, James, *General Butler in New Orleans.* Mason Brothers, 1864.

Poore, Ben Perley, *The Life and Public Services of Ambrose E. Burnside: Soldier-Citizen-Statesman.* J. A. & R. A. Reid, Publishers, 1882.

Reed, Rowena, *Combined Operations in the Civil War.* Naval Institute Press, 1978.

Rhett, Robert Goodwyn, *Charleston: An Epic of Carolina.* Garrett and Massie, Incorporated, 1940.

Ripley, Warren, *Artillery and Ammunition of the Civil War.* Van Nostrand Reinhold Company, 1970.

Robinson, Frank T., *History of the Fifth Regiment, M.V.M.* W. F. Brown & Company, Printers, 1879.

Roe, Alfred S., *The Fifth Regiment: Massachusetts Volunteer Infantry.* Fifth Regiment Veteran Association, 1911.

Scharf, J. Thomas, *History of the Confederate States Navy.* The Fairfax Press, 1977.

Soley, James Russell, *Admiral Porter.* D. Appleton and Company, 1903.

Spears, John Randolph, *David G. Farragut.* George W. Jacobs & Company, 1905.

Stearns, William Augustus, *Adjutant Stearns.* Massachusetts Sabbath School Society, 1862.

Stevens, Hazard, *The Life of Isaac Ingalls Stevens,* Vol. 2. Houghton, Mifflin and Company, 1900.

Still, William N., Jr., *Iron Afloat: The Story of the Confederate Armorclads.* Vanderbilt University Press, 1971.

Tucker, Glenn, *Zeb Vance: Champion of Personal Freedom.* The Bobbs-Merrill Company, Inc., 1965.

United States Navy Department, *Official Records of the Union and Confederate Navies in the War of the Rebellion.* U.S. Government Printing Office, 1906.

United States War Department, *The War of the Rebellion: A Compilation of the Official Records of the Union and Confederate Armies.* U.S. Government Printing Office, 1902.

Walcott, Charles F., *History of the Twenty-First Regiment Massachusetts Volunteers in the War for the Preservation of the Union, 1861-1865.* Houghton, Mifflin and Company, 1882.

Warner, Ezra J.:
Generals in Blue: Lives of the Union Commanders. Louisiana State University Press, 1964.

Generals in Gray: Lives of the Confederate Commanders. Louisiana State University Press, 1959.

Welles, Gideon, *Diary of Gideon Welles*, Vol. 1. Houghton Mifflin Company, 1911.

West, Richard S., Jr.:
Mr. Lincoln's Navy. Longmans Green and Company, 1957.
The Second Admiral: A Life of David Dixon Porter, 1813-1891. Coward-McCann, Inc., 1937.

Whitman, George Washington, *Civil War Letters of George Washington Whitman.* Ed. by Jerome M. Loving. Duke University Press, 1975.

Williams, T. Harry, *P.G.T. Beauregard: Napoleon in Gray.* Louisiana State University Press, 1955.

Winters, John D., *The Civil War in Louisiana.* Louisiana State University Press, 1963.

Yearns, W. Buck, and John G. Barrett, eds., *North Carolina Civil War Documentary.* The University of North Carolina Press, 1980.

Other Sources

Bassham, Ben L., "Conrad Chapman's Charleston." *Civil War Times Illustrated,* April 1977.

Cable, George W., "New Orleans before the Capture." *The Century Illustrated Monthly Magazine,* April 1885.

"Conrad Wise Chapman: The Artist's Early Years." *The Museum of the Confederacy Newsletter,* Spring/Summer 1982.

"Conrad Wise Chapman: An Exhibition of His Works in the Valentine Museum," Valentine Museum, 1962.

Elrod, Mark, "Military Bands and Bandsmen, 1861-1865." *Military Images Magazine,* November/December 1983.

Julian, Allen P., "Fort Pulaski." *Civil War Times Illustrated,* May 1970.

Luvaas, Jay, "Burnside's Roanoke Island Campaign." *Civil War Times Illustrated,* December 1968.

Thomas, Emory M., "The Lost Confederates of Roanoke." *Civil War Times Illustrated,* May 1976.

Tyler, W. S., "A Memorial of Adj. Frazar A. Stearns, of the 21st Massachusetts Volunteers, Killed at Newbern, March 14, 1862." Amherst College, 1862.

Welles, Gideon, "Admiral Farragut and New Orleans." *The Galaxy,* November and December 1871.

PICTURE CREDITS

The sources for the illustrations in this book are shown below. Credits from left to right are separated by semicolons, from top to bottom by dashes.

Cover: Painting by M.F.H. de Haas, courtesy The Historic New Orleans Collection, 533 Royal Street, photographed by Jan White (Acc. No. 1974.80). 2, 3: Map by Peter McGinn. 8, 9: Samuel H. Lockett Papers, #432, Southern Historical Collection, Library of the University of North Carolina at Chapel Hill, copied by Chip Henderson, except top right, P. K. Yonge Library of Florida History, University of Florida, Gainesville. 10, 11: From *The Photographic History of the Civil War,* ed. Francis Trevelyan Miller, © 1911 Patriot Publishing Co., Springfield, Mass.; Samuel H. Lockett Papers, #432, Southern Historical Collection, Library of the University of North Carolina at Chapel Hill, copied by Chip Henderson. 12, 13: Florida Photographic Collection, Florida State Archives, inset, from *The Photographic History of the Civil War,* ed. Francis Trevelyan Miller, © 1911 Patriot Publishing Co., Springfield, Mass. 14, 15: From *The Photographic History of the Civil War,* ed. Francis Trevelyan Miller, © 1911 Patriot Publishing Co., Springfield, Mass. 18, 19: Drawing by Alfred R. Waud, courtesy Franklin D. Roosevelt Library. 20: Courtesy The New-York Historical Society, New York City. 22, 23: Courtesy Frank & Marie-T. Wood Print Collections, Alexandria, Virginia. 25: U.S. Naval History Center, Department of the Navy — National Archives Neg. No. 111-B-2802. 26, 27: Courtesy The New-York Historical Society, New York City, inset, from *Official Records of the Union and Confederate Navies in the War of the Rebellion,* Vol. 6, Washington, D.C., 1897. 28, 29: Courtesy Frank & Marie-T. Wood Print Collections, Alexandria, Virginia, insets, National Archives Neg. No. 111-B-5886; Library of Congress. 31: Courtesy Frank & Marie-T. Wood Print Collections, Alexandria, Virginia. 32: National Archives Neg. Nos. 111-B-6073; 165-JT-224 — 111-BA-534. 33: Painting by Vincent Colyer, courtesy private collection. 34: From *A Memorial of Adj. Frazar A. Stearns* by The Rev. W. S. Tyler, Printed for the Junior Class of Amherst College. 36: Courtesy Frank & Marie-T. Wood Print Collections, Alexandria, Virginia — Library of Congress. 38, 39: Courtesy Frank & Marie-T. Wood Print Collections, Alexandria, Virginia. 40-42: New Hampshire Historical Society. 43-45: Western Reserve Historical Society, Cleveland, Ohio. 46, 47: Courtesy National Park Service, Fort Pulaski National Monument, courtesy The New-York Historical Society, New York City. 48, 49: Library of Congress. 50, 51: Courtesy National Park Service, Fort Pulaski National Monument. 52, 53: Western Reserve Historical Society, Cleveland, Ohio. 55: Chicago Historical Society No. 1920.1078. 56, 57: Courtesy The Historic New Orleans Collection, 533 Royal Street (Acc. No. 1982.32.1). 58: Library of Congress. 59: National Archives Neg. No. 111-B-513. 60: National Archives Neg. No. 111-B-5889. 61: Chicago Historical Society Neg. No. ICHi-11580. 62: Map by Walter W. Roberts. 65: Courtesy Frank & Marie-T. Wood Print Collections, Alexandria, Virginia. 66: Courtesy The New-York Historical Society, New York City. 68: Courtesy The Historic New Orleans Collection, 533 Royal Street (Acc. No. OS 47-4-L). 69: Courtesy Frank & Marie-T. Wood Print Collections, Alexandria, Virginia. 70: From *The Photographic History of the Civil War,* ed. Francis Trevelyan Miller, © 1911 Patriot Publishing Co., Springfield, Mass. — Department of Archives and Manuscripts, Louisiana State University, Baton Rouge. 71: U.S. Army Military History Institute, copied by Robert Walch — *Civil War Times Illustrated* Collection. 72: Library of Congress. 73: Courtesy Frank & Marie-T. Wood Print Collections, Alexandria, Virginia. 75: Painting by Julian Oliver Davidson, courtesy American Heritage Picture Collection. 76: Museum of the Confederacy, Richmond, Virginia — The W. S. Hoole Special Collections Library, University of Alabama. 78, 79: National Archives RG 156, Entry 201, Vol. 3, p. 106; courtesy Thomas S. Dickey, photographed by Michael W. Thomas. 80, 81: Courtesy The Brady Collection, National Archives; U.S. Army Military History Institute, copied by Robert Walch — courtesy Thomas S. Dickey, photographed by Michael W. Thomas (3). 82, 83: Western Reserve Historical Society, Cleveland, Ohio; Library of Congress — courtesy Thomas S. Dickey, photographed by Michael W. Thomas (5). 85: Courtesy Hall of Flags, State House, Boston, photographed by Jack Leonard. 87: National Archives Neg. No. 111-B-4145. 88, 89: U.S. Army Military History Institute, copied by Robert Walch. 91: Painting by Harry M. Wegner, courtesy Virginia Historical Society, photographed by George Nan. 92: Courtesy Frank & Marie-T. Wood Print Collections, Alexandria, Virginia. 93: Map by Walter W. Roberts. 94: Western Reserve Historical Society, Cleveland, Ohio. 96: From *The Photographic History of the Civil War,* ed. Francis Trevelyan Miller, © 1911 Patriot Publishing Co., Springfield, Mass. 98-109: Paintings by Conrad Wise Chapman, courtesy Museum of the Confederacy, Richmond, Virginia, photographed by Larry Sherer. 111: National Archives Neg. No. 165-C-799. 112: National Archives Neg. No. 111-B-1233. 113: Map by Walter W. Roberts. 114: From *The Photographic History of the Civil War,* ed. Francis Trevelyan Miller, © 1911 Patriot Publishing Co., Springfield, Mass. 115: Courtesy Eleutherian Mills Historical Library. 116, 117: Courtesy The New-York Historical Society, New York City. 119: Courtesy Frank & Marie-T. Wood Print Collections, Alexandria, Virginia. 120: National Archives Neg. No. 111-B-1201. 121: U.S. Army Military History Institute, copied by Robert Walch. 122, 123: Library of Congress. 124: Virginia State Library — courtesy Brian Pohanka. 125: Courtesy The New-York Historical Society, New York City. 126: Sculpture by Augustus Saint-Gaudens, City of Boston Art Commission, photographed by Jack Leonard. 127: From *History of the Fifty-Fourth Regiment of Massachusetts Volunteer Infantry, 1863-1865,* by Luis Fenollosa Emilio, The Boston Book Company, 1894 — Private collection, photographed by Nick Whitman. 128: U.S. Army Military History Institute, copied by Robert Walch. 129: Library of Congress. 130, 131: Courtesy Frank & Marie-T. Wood Print Collections, Alexandria, Virginia. 132, 133: Library of Congress; U.S. Army Military History Institute, copied by Robert Walch. 135: U.S. Army Military History Institute, copied by Robert Walch. 136: Courtesy Frank & Marie-T. Wood Print Collections, Alexandria, Virginia. 137: Library of Congress. 138: Painting by Conrad Wise Chapman, courtesy Museum of the Confederacy, Richmond, Virginia, photographed by Larry Sherer — Naval Historical Center, Department of the Navy, courtesy General Dynamics Corp., Electric Boat Division. 140, 141: National Archives Neg. No. 165-C-752. 143: Courtesy Steven J. Selenfriend, photographed by Al Freni. 144, 145: Courtesy The Mariners' Museum, Newport News, Virginia; courtesy Charles V. Peery, Charleston, South Carolina. 146: Naval History Center, Department of the Navy. 148, 149: Painting by Julian Oliver Davidson, courtesy The New-York Historical Society, New York City. 150: Library of Congress. 152: Courtesy Frank & Marie-T. Wood Print Collections, Alexandria, Virginia; West Point Museum, U.S. Military Academy, photographed by Henry Groskinsky. 153: West Point Museum, U.S. Military Academy, photographed by Henry Groskinsky. 154, 155: Painting by William Heysham Overend, courtesy The Wadsworth Atheneum, Hartford, Gift of the Citizens of Hartford by subscription, May 24, 1886, photographed by Al Freni. 157: Michigan Department of State, State Archives Neg. No. 01072. 159: Courtesy Frank & Marie-T. Wood Print Collections, Alexandria, Virginia. 160, 161: Courtesy Beverley R. Robinson Collection, U.S. Naval Academy Museum, Annapolis, Maryland. 162: Museum of the Confederacy, Richmond, Virginia. 163: Library of Congress. 165: U.S. Army Military History Institute, copied by Robert Walch. 166, 167: Courtesy Beverley R. Robinson Collection, U.S. Naval Academy Museum, Annapolis, Maryland. 168-171: Library of Congress.

INDEX